WORKPLACE RECOGNITION
Step-by-step examples of a positive reinforcement strategy

WORKPLACE RECOGNITION

Step-by-step examples of a positive reinforcement strategy

SUE GLASSCOCK & KIMBERLY GRAM

Meaning, Myths, Methods and Magic

B. T. BATSFORD LTD • LONDON & WASHINGTON

© Sue Glasscock, Kimberly Gram, 1999

First published in 1999

Published by B T Batsford Ltd.
583 Fulham Road
LONDON, SW6 5BY

Printed by WBC Book Manufacturers
Bridgend
Wales

Batsford Business Online: www.batsford.com

British Library Cataloguing in Publication Data

ISBN 0 7134 8561 2

All rights reserved. Unauthorised duplication by any
means contravenes applicable laws.
Sue Glassock and Kimberly Gram have asserted their
moral right under the Copyright, Designs and Patents
Act, 1988, to be indentified as Authors of this Work.

A CIP catalogue record for this book is available from
The British Library

**This book is dedicated with the deepest love
and the greatest appreciation
to those whose love and support
enriches our lives on a daily basis -**

*Jim Glasscock
Gene Stefanski
Jack and Peggy Gram
Leon and Helen Shafer
&
Dustin, Jessica, Todd, Beau, Kelly and Tyler*

CONTENTS

INTRODUCTION

What's in It for Me?	11
Assessing Your Recognition Effectiveness	35

Section 1: MEANING

What Recognition Really Means	43
Recognition and Reward Are Not Synonymous!	59
Positive Reinforcement - The Scientific Evidence	65
The Flip Side - Negative Reinforcement and Negative Consequences	71
What Do the Experts Say?	77

Section 2: MYTHS

Myth #1: Cash Is The Best Recognition Method	83
Myth #2: A Salary Is Enough	87
Myth #3: Employee Competition Brings Out the Best in Our People	91
Myth #4: Only Star Performers Deserve Recognition	97
What Isn't Recognition	101

Section 3: METHODS

Developing Your Unique Recognition Strategy	107
Step One: Determine What You Want to Achieve	109
Step Two: Identify What You Will Recognize	117
Step Three: Select Your Recognition Tools	127

Section 4: MAGIC

Step Four: Show You Care	147
Implementation Tips	153
The Magician	161
Step Five: Measure, Monitor and Continuously Improve Your Recognition Processes	167
Potential Benefits of Effective Recognition Systems	171

CLOSING THOUGHTS

"Caring"	177
Acknowledgments	189
Bibliography	193
Index	195

Introduction

*You have to have your heart in your business
and the business in your heart.*

Thomas J. Watson, Sr.

What's in it for me?

"Never doubt that a small group of thoughtful, committed people can change the world; indeed it is the only thing that ever has."

Margaret Mead

RECOGNITION is very simply the positive reinforcement methods we use in the workplace. Positive reinforcement is a subject which has been seriously researched by scientists for over 80 years in hundreds of different published studies. And, the good news is the results have been confirmed over and over again, and the lessons learned are directly applicable in the workplace. The bad news is we're not paying attention! Human behavior, after all, impacts every goal, decision, relationship and activity we have at work. So, why aren't we studying it?

Reinforcement methods are based in science – they are factual and can be proven. Unfortunately, somewhere along the line, American business labeled and treated recognition as an employee benefit, rendering it ineffective as a positive reinforcement tool. When used effectively, recognition is much more than a nice thing to do for employees, it is the most powerful tool at our disposal. Regardless of whether we are trying to improve individual or company performance, to enhance teamwork, to build long-lasting partnerships with our customers and suppliers or to reach our goals successfully and in record time, positive reinforcement is the best tool to facilitate our efforts.

An effective recognition system can be used to teach a new behavior or practice or to change an existing behavior or practice. Our marketplace demands that we have the ability to change quickly and dramatically. Since there is evidence that positive reinforcement is much more effective than negative reinforcement and punishment in teaching and driving long-term change, we need to have an effective recognition system in order to ensure our competitiveness. Are any of the following items part of your business plan:

- ✓ Improving communications?
- ✓ Building relationships and loyalty in your professional network – customers, suppliers, subordinates, superiors and peers?
- ✓ Driving change and decreasing the time it takes to achieve goals?
- ✓ Ensuring that corporate values are demonstrated?
- ✓ Reducing attrition rates?
- ✓ Unleashing the untapped potential for creativity and goal achievement in your employees?

If so, the key to success is implementation of an effective workplace recognition system.

Many of us believe that we have good recognition systems in place. Ask yourself the following questions :

- ✓ Is your employee recognition system based on a competition?
- ✓ Is less than 100% of your employee population recognized annually?
- ✓ Is your recognition system based on cash rewards?
- ✓ Is recognition an event that occurs once a year?
- ✓ Are your recognition tools management driven?
- ✓ Is your recognition system "one size fits all"?

If you answered "yes" to any of these questions, the system you are using is NOT effective recognition and should be analyzed and improved so that you realize the greatest impact for your investment.

IMPROVING COMMUNICATIONS

"A man on a mission is far different than a drone on a deadline."

Rheta Grimsley Johnson

If we expect our employee population to stay focused on what is good for our business, we must clearly define the path we wish to follow. Without clear communication, the ability to execute our plans and achieve our goals is questionable at best. We have adopted several new and improved "communication" methods to make our work life easier. Take a moment to consider the "communication" you experienced during the last week. Many of you probably "communicated" using the following tools:

- FAX
- "Voice mail purgatory"
- Electronic mail
- Automatic banking transaction
- Computer network message
- Interoffice memo
- Form letter.

The word "communication" comes from the same Latin root word as community and communion. The Latin word meant "to participate or mutual participation". Not one of the above tools requires the personal contact suggested by "mutual participation". What are we sacrificing by eliminating this personal contact? Do we really want our work life to be this impersonal? Are we becoming ineffective communicators? Is this just another case of schedule taking precedence over quality?

These examples and more illustrate how we have isolated ourselves from human contact and relationships. United Airlines has a television commercial which emphasizes how the airline had lost an old customer by growing too impersonal in its "communications". As a result of the feedback, the manager is distributing tickets to his employees to personally visit their customers. The last ticket is his, to visit the customer that was lost. The methods mentioned above have supposedly made us "more efficient communicators". They are cheaper and faster than other options. But, if we solely depend on these methods, what will replace our innate need for human contact, the benefits we gain from investing in personal relationships with our customers and employees, and our business requirement of communicating a consistent message on our corporate direction?

John Naisbitt, author of the book *Megatrends*, states: "We must learn to balance the material wonders of technology with the spiritual demands of our natures". Superior customer partnerships and outstanding professional relationships are achieved by positive and personal interactions with others. We are social creatures. So, while these high technology communication tools have become the norm, we still possess our human need to have positive, in-person communication with others.

In *The Habit of Communication* published by the Covey Leadership Center in 1995, the authors report that communications experts estimate that only 10 percent of our communication is represented by the words we say, another 30 percent by our sound or tone and 60 percent by our body language. This makes me wonder just how effective our new communication techniques can be if only 10 percent of our message is being received. Take the form letter as an example. I get "form letters" from Ed McMahon – did you know he wants me to win the sweepstakes? NOT! This method is not effective in our personal lives, so why do we pretend that we can fool people in the workplace? And, what is your first clue in your personal relationships that someone values you and cares about you? You see it in their eyes, you hear it in their voice, you witness it in their actions. If we are going to be successful communicators in the workplace, we need to ensure personal contact with our customers, our employees and those in our professional networks.

Positive interactions and experiences are a form of positive reinforcement. Most businesses never miss an opportunity to show appreciation to their customers. This same habit must be translated into our other professional relationships – those with suppliers, management, subordinates, peers and other functions within our companies. As with customers, these relationships require that we never miss an opportunity to listen and to show our appreciation, the two most valuable communication skills.

BUILDING RELATIONSHIPS

"Relationships are the currency of the future."

"Relationships require trust; trust is at the core of every loyal relationship."

ONE SIZE FITS ONE
Gary Heil, Tom Parker & Deborah C. Stephens

Consider the things we have done to make our work life easier. We have our personal computers, state-of-the-art copiers, thousands of forms and standard documents . . . every high-tech appliance and piece of paper one could ask for (maybe a few hundred extras!). We have government controls on our safety, employment, environment, health and so forth. There are ergonomically correct chairs, work-stations and keyboards. What could possibly be missing from this picture of a wonderful work environment? Perhaps trust, respect, dignity, self-worth, warmth, sincerity and all of those interpersonal qualities that evolve from investing in long-term mutually beneficial relationships. Are these investments too "inefficient" for these times?

Stephen Covey, in ***Seven Habits of Highly Effective People***, talks about a P/PC principle (production/production capability) as it applies to organizational effectiveness. He states:

*"There are organizations that talk a lot about the customer and then completely neglect the people that deal with the customer – the employees. The PC principle is to always treat your employees **exactly** as you want them to treat your best customers.*

"You can buy a person's hand, but you can't buy his heart. His heart is where his enthusiasm is, his loyalty. You can buy his back,

but you can't buy his brain. That's where his creativity is, his ingenuity, his resourcefulness.

"PC is treating employees as volunteers just as you treat your customers as volunteers, because that's what they are. They volunteer their best parts – their hearts and minds."

Why do we abandon the practice of sincere appreciation when we come to work? Saying "thank you" is much more than a social amenity – it is an extremely valuable business tool. Tom Peters dedicated one entire syndicated business column to saying "thank you." He states:

"The handwritten thank you is a modest engagement. It probably won't save lives, but it just might boost your odds of becoming rich, famous and adored. (Not to mention making you feel a lot better about yourself)".

He shares the story of a former manager who religiously spent 15 minutes at the end of each day to write about a half-dozen paragraph-long notes to people who had given him time during the day or made a provocative remark in a meeting. Peters shares that this manager became a highly-successful CEO during the course of his career. The article challenges the reader to try this end-of-the-day ritual for one month, guaranteeing "amazing" results.

Recognition plays an important role for all of us. It is important that we give and receive recognition for steady consistent efforts, as well as outstanding efforts. Success should be celebrated for meeting expected goals and for accomplishing the unexpected. Recognition is very emotional and personal for both the giver and the receiver. For this reason, our intent is to help you establish a framework that allows all employees to participate in the recognition process. You must implement the processes, methods and tools needed to give the heartfelt, warm and immediate appreciation that will encourage and reinforce the personal attributes individuals need to be creative and innovative, to operate at their highest possible performance level, and to have pride and celebrate their work contributions.

What about our customer relationships? Using personal experience, start by trying to define a "superior customer relationship". If we look at the word "relationship", it comes from the same Latin root as the word relative. The definition of relationship uses words such as kinship and binding partnership. Relationship insinuates a personal knowledge and loyalty to someone. Who do you purchase goods and services from that fits this category? Some individuals may come to mind immediately – your hairdresser/barber, Avon representative, mechanic, doctor and lawyer. In these dealings, there is usually one person you choose to deal with and trust. These are people that treat you respectfully, fairly, ethically and, even though you pay for their services, you consider them friends (they are on my Christmas card list).

We also are aware of our own negative experiences as customers. There are several things that bother me in my role as customer including:

- I absolutely hate not being able to talk to a human being and the requirement of punching 100 numbers into a telephone system just to get to the wrong person – so computerized phone systems would have to top my list.
- There is nothing worse than trying to correct a mistake on a bill.
- I miss going to a department store and having a sales person say, "Can I help you find something?" It seems like the malls are staffed by teenagers, who I consider to be the communication challenge of the century.
- Does anyone miss full service gas stations? I loved having my oil, tires and washer fluid checked, and getting the windshield cleaned. I guess the oil companies figure they are getting off cheap by paying just one person minimum wage to work the station. But, what are they losing in "suggestive sales", such as a quart of oil, washer fluid, etc., and how loyal can we be to a business which has a different person behind the cash drawer every week?

- And, there is the awful experience of needing to exchange an item – the store know it is their merchandise from the bar coding, but many require the receipt, my name, my address, my phone number, two forms of identification and 30 - 45 minutes of my time to get $3 back.

Since we are all customers, it is fairly easy to figure out what actions make customers loyal – high quality, fair price, personal service, respect, etc. When one or more of these expected attributes are missing, the result is an unhappy customer, which is very costly to the supplier of the product or service. Consider the following statistics on unhappy customers:

- It costs five times more to develop a new customer than to keep an old one.
- It cost 11 times more to recapture a dissatisfied customer than it does to maintain an existing relationship.
- Only 4% of dissatisfied customers complain; the other 96% just quietly go away and 91% will never come back to your business.
- Dissatisfied customers will tell eight to ten people about you and, if the customer is up to speed on the Internet, they can ruin you globally in a matter of seconds.
- Seven out of ten complaining customers will continue to do business with you if you resolve the complaint in their favor; 95% if you resolve the complaint on the spot.

The dictionary definition of "customer" is "a person one has to deal with", and "one that patronizes or uses the services of someone or something". This really broadens our perspective. These definitions encompass every one you talk to and work with every day. What if my *modus operandi* at work became "How can I help?" instead of "No," "I can't," "It's not my job!" and the rest of the excuses we all have used? What if you treated every one you deal with the way you would treat your best external customer, as if your paycheck and future depended on how you interacted? What if you conducted your work as if your nearest and dearest was going to receive the product? You probably would make sure it was the best it could be, the most reasonable price, on time – heck! you might even wrap it up with a ribbon and a card.

Recently, at Village Inn, the wait staff were wearing big bright buttons that said, "We're Number Two!" Of course, your first reaction is that Denny's or Perkins has overtaken them in the marketplace, so you ask, "Who is Number One?" The response is, "You are". I laughed so hard when the waitress said it, but you know, that silly button started up the conversation and clearly stated their value, "Our customers are our top priority!"

In a **Business Week** on-line interview conducted in May 1995, Gary Hamel stated, *"I don't believe you can expect employees to have substantially better relationships with customers than management has with employees. If there's a lot of cynicism, it's going to filter down through to customers."* Reaffirming this, a conference speaker from the Ritz-Carlton Hotel recently made the statement, *"There is less to fear from outside competition than inside inefficiency, discourtesy and bad service."*

This is true for all business and industry. The way we treat our employees and peers in the workplace is often directly reflected in our customer relationships. We need to positively reinforce the behaviors and activities that build superior relationships inside and outside of our company walls, so that we ensure best practices in customer service. We cannot depend on our sales force and our marketing group to achieve "superior customer relationships". It must be everyone's responsibility. The buck stops here in our own backyard. Customer expectations change by the minute, so our job descriptions will never be accurate – we need to be flexible, remember our manners and assume our position as "#2" in the food chain. We need to eliminate "no" and "I can't" from our vocabulary, consider complaints as gifts/opportunities/challenges and every time we encounter a work associate immediately think , "my business and paycheck depends on this relationship," and ask - "Can I help you?"

The first step in establishing the relationships that are essential to our success is to develop a system to recognize and positively reinforce each other at work. Having training and tools in place serves as a reminder that our relationships in the workplace are a top priority. It not only helps us build these relationships and reach goals, but it is critical to sustaining motivation and the quality of work life. It helps make work not only bearable, but enjoyable. The more that recognition is woven into our work days, the more its results will positively impact customer relationships, productivity, profitability and morale.

DRIVING CHANGE IN PHILOSOPHY, BEHAVIORS, PRACTICES AND PERFORMANCE

"You must be the change you want to see in the world."

Mohandas Ghandi

Ask any successful parent, schoolteacher, coach or psychologist. Positive and immediate reinforcement is the key to changing an existing behavior or teaching a new one. Human beings respond to appreciation, acknowledgment and approval. People ARE a company's most valuable resource. The quality of work life should be our top priority and the personal responsibility of every individual in the workplace. We must stop changing hats in the workplace, for we still possess all of our basic needs when we are at work. We cannot abandon the innate need to feel noticed and appreciated at the company's front door.

Robert Frost once said *"The brain is a wonderful organ; it starts working the moment you get up in the morning and does not stop until you get to the office."* This is especially true when it comes to positive reinforcement. The ingredients are not magical or a mystery to any of us. Most of us have applied these recognition techniques outside of the workplace. For example:

- Training the family dog
- Potty-training our children
- Coaching a child's sports team
- Thanking a friend or relative for a gift

- Teaching a class or being a student
- Participating in Scouts.

All of these personal activities involve the use of positive reinforcement to change or encourage a behavior or skill. In most cases, the positive reinforcement is simply sincere appreciation accompanied with a small token – a dog biscuit, a popsicle, a hug, a trophy, a thank you note, a smiley face sticker or a merit badge. Not one of these tokens of appreciation is extravagant, yet each has very effectively facilitated learning. This shows there is truth to the old adage *"It is not the gift, it's the thought that counts"*.

Establishing an effective recognition system is vital to positively reinforcing the behaviors and activities necessary to achieve the personal principles and practices required to be a viable and successful business operation. There are many new management and work initiatives to help us improve productivity, drive change and enhance quality. Frankly, implementing any new initiative is a challenge that cannot be met efficiently and effectively without the proper recognition system. In most situations, we have the same "players" but an entirely different "ball game". We know these approaches are the right way to operate. We know we will reap great benefits. In order to get from "here to there" and implement the new strategies and methods of operation which will keep our businesses competitive, we need to train in appropriate relationship skills and techniques, and equip ourselves with the knowledge and tools for effective recognition.

There is a wonderful book on positive reinforcement by Aubrey C. Daniels, entitled ***Bringing Out the Best in People - How to Apply the Astonishing Power of Positive Reinforcement***, which we highly recommend to anyone wishing to manage performance or drive change. The most important lesson learned from this book is that WE ARE NOT ADVERSE TO CHANGE! We have heard the following statements so many times – "People resist change" or "Nobody likes change" – we are totally convinced that human beings hate change. But, guess what? After all of these years, we discover that there is scientific evidence that WE CAN CHANGE. Daniels states *"People don't resist change if the change provides immediate positive consequences for them"*. Initially, we felt a little foolish for not realizing this intuitively. We had, after all, effectively used positive reinforcement in many of our personal and professional interactions. But, considering that American industry has paid millions for consultants, books and training on change management, we felt a little better. Two of the reasons Daniels feels we are ineffective at driving change are that the immediate consequences are negative and that we attempt to manage by simply telling people what to do. Some examples of this ineffectiveness might be:

Example One

Mary works on the sales floor on Monday through Friday. One of her annual goals was to increase her sales by 10% which she has accomplished in less than three months . Her boss calls her into the office and says "Mary, you have done incredibly well in a short period of time." Mary beams with pride and delight. Then, her boss says "I work my best sales people on weekends when we have the biggest customer turnout, so I have changed your work schedule". Mary has children; she has no day care on weekends and she wants to actively participate in their extra curricular activities – soccer and baseball – which occur on Saturday mornings. Is this change going to be difficult for Mary? Yes, the immediate consequences for improved performance are negative for her.

Daniels cites the fact that, most of the time, individuals resist new corporate initiatives because the immediate consequences of doing things differently are all negative – they require extra effort to learn, result in increased mistakes orincreased paperwork, require time away from the job causing the individual to get behind in their other tasks. Immediate consequences are the most influential of all reinforcement types and are directly tied to how we behave.

Example Two

A manufacturing manager announces that the department

must reduce cycle time by 10% in the next 12 months. One month goes by and the cycle time stays the same. He decides to post a large chart in the middle of the area to re-emphasize the goal. Two months go by – nothing. He decides to call a special meeting to reiterate the importance of the goal. He shares how he will not get his management bonus if this goal is not achieved. Three months pass and no reaction or improvement. Finally, he tells his reports that every time they are able to shave 2% off of the cycle time and maintain the level for a month, they will all leave early on Friday and he will buy pizza. The first month, the cycle time reduces 4%.

Daniels calls the first part of this manager's approach the "louder, longer, meaner" method. We barrage people with memos, letters, news articles, wall hangings, speeches, meetings, policies, etc. This never works, as human beings, in general, do not do what they are told unless there are immediate consequences associated with the change. Daniels gives the example of the health warning on a package of cigarettes – has everyone quit smoking? Telling someone to do something is an "antecedent" which should always be paired with immediate, consistent and meaningful consequences. Telling people over and over again does not work. Promises of a great future do not work. Threats not followed with immediate consequences do not work. You must have both immediate positive reinforcement and negative consequences associated with the behavior change.

Daniels states:

> *"People do what they do because of what happens to them when they do it. And, the more immediately the consequence occurs, the more likely you are to see a change. . . Consequently, the one thing executives, managers and supervisors should know the most about is the science of human behavior. The behavior of people is the only way anything is accomplished in business. Human performance is*

not a factor in a complicated equation for business success; it is the answer to the equation."

So, the next time you think another person is being "unwilling to change" or "resistant to change," or you are having trouble motivating your employees to achieve goals, you must remember to consider that human beings are constantly and continuously changing, by the day, the hour, the minute, even the nanosecond. Human beings love change! Human beings are change experts! And then, ask yourself, "What consequences did I fail to provide to effectively facilitate the change?"

ENSURING VALUES

"You can't buy people's time; you can buy their physical presence at a given place; you can even buy a measured number of their muscular motions per hour. But you cannot buy enthusiasm . . . you cannot buy loyalty . . . you cannot buy the devotion of their hearts. You must earn these."

Rev Dr Martin Luther King. Jr.

The majority of us spend over one-half of our waking hours at work. Unfortunately, most of us undergo a personality change as soon as we arrive at work. Our job descriptions do not call for common sense, common courtesy, honesty, sincerity, gratitude or being personable, so we abandon these personal attributes in the parking lot. Most corporate strategic goals do not include quality of work life plans to drive improvement in employee satisfaction, morale, the attrition rate or the work environment. Do we think that creativity, loyalty, dependability, trustworthiness and initiative are of a lower priority than stock prices, market share, the reliability of our products, the quality of our services and the cycle time of our processes? Do we think by establishing these tangible corporate goals, the values and principles required of the workforce will naturally follow? Maybe we think competitive compensation packages will ensure these personal attributes or that we can buy the personal qualities required by a successful business operation. But, these "personal" processes are no different than any other corporate process and result. Recognition, like all other corporate processes, requires constant attention, improvement, monitoring and maintenance (plan, do, check, act). As with any personal relationship, building effective relationships with suppliers, customers, peers, management, subordinates, benchmarking partners and our professional networks requires constant care to guarantee success. Effective recognition is critical to creating an environment that breeds creativity, innovation and mutual respect.

In ***Built To Last - Successful Habits of Visionary Companies*** by James C. Collins and Jerry I. Porras, the authors state *"Contrary to business school doctrine, we did not find 'maximizing shareholder wealth' or 'profit maximization' as the dominant driving force or primary objective through the history of most visionary companies (17 out of 18 of the most visionary and successful US companies were more ideologically driven and less purely profit driven)."* These visionary companies have a cluster of objectives; they seek profits, but they are equally guided by a higher sense of purpose and a required code of conduct. They strive for results, but concentrate equally on "how the goal is achieved." In most cases, these visionary companies make more money than those companies which are solely "money driven".

Another study, the Yankelovich Survey, revealed that, by a 3 to 1 margin, Americans believe businesses have a greater obligation to their employees than to their bottom line. Because American industry has begun to recognize the importance of establishing an ideology, many have attempted to fill the void by establishing a set of corporate values. Core values are usually a list of behaviors and practices that provide a code of ethics or behavioral framework for all of our work actions. A list of values is meaningless without a reinforcement system which includes positive reinforcement for those who exemplify and live the values and negative consequences for those who do not. Most corporate values are well-written and thoroughly communicated, but recent surveys have found that it is a rare company today in which people are "practicing what they preach". The level of management commitment to values can be seen by witnessing the consequences of both living the values and what occurs when an individual purposely acts in a manner inconsistent with the values. Obviously, it takes more than a statement or posting of intent, to inculcate company values into our work culture. The only thing worse than not having values is to say you have values that you do not adhere to. People would much rather see a sermon than to hear one.

Each of us knows that there is a big difference in our work between the times when we "have to do" a task and when we "want to do" a task. It is the difference between "good enough" and exceptional performance, run-of-the-mill and top-of-the-line, same solutions and innovative approaches. In addition, there is a difference in our work when someone is paying attention to us and when no one notices our efforts (i.e. the Hawthorne effect). We need to stop treating our work associates like they are only a "pair of hands" and a mind. We must bring the "spirit" back into the workplace. All of our efforts are wasted, if the spirit is missing.

In *One Size Fits One*, by Gary Heil, Tom Parker and Deborah C. Stephens, the authors state

> *"When the people we (customers) deal with demonstrate a love and interest for their work, their spirit is infectious, and the possibility of gaining our loyalty is greatly improved. On the other hand, if the people we work with seem merely to be going through the motions, no matter how empowered they are or how much information they have for us, their lackluster attitude won't buy their company much more than the bare minimum of our attention, and little if any of our loyalty. If the people we do business with communicate an excitement for their work and for building our relationship, we'll go out of our way to find a reason to continue to work with them. Spirit is like a magnet. If it's there in the companies we do business with, we'll be attracted to it – just like we are to the college football team, the actress, the politician, or any individual with spirit."*

This spirit, excitement, loyalty and love for work can be achieved when we make the decision that they are the top priority and the key ingredients to our success and future. These attributes can be achieved by identifying what is really important to us (the business and its employees) and our customers, communicating these objectives and by having the recognition system in place to immediately and continuously reinforce our priorities.

A new theory on leadership has emerged in the 90s. It states that management should not be rated and compensated for the business goals, which their people actually achieve, but for their leadership skills – motivating people to their highest performance levels and creating an environment which encourages mutual respect, trust, innovation, pride and loyalty. In *One Size Fits One*, the authors state, *"We're convinced that the way a company treats its employees will filter down to the way those employees treat us (the customer)."* With the global nature and size of our businesses, however, managers often have subordinates in different buildings, states, countries and continents. So, in addition to the new evaluation practice, we believe that recognition and positive reinforcement should be a skill that each of us has in the workplace. The quality of work life and our work relationships should be the responsibility of all. By making everyone accountable, we could avoid the following mistakes:

✓ Upon completion of a major project on which one employee expended all of her "blood, sweat and tears" for no personal credit, she waited patiently for a simple thanks from the boss. One week went by. Two weeks went by, and still there was no notice, compliments or tokens of emotional support. Finally, in a staff meeting, the boss enthusiastically spoke of the positive feedback received on the project and recognized another individual on the staff for the accomplishment. The employee thought that the manager was a "good" person with good intentions, but the truth was after working three years in the same department, she did not know! About 99.8% of what the manager thought of the employee's performance was expressed during an annual performance evaluation. It was obvious there was some confusion over who was doing what. Unfortunately, this type of work interaction is not the exception, it is the general rule.

✓ Another well-meaning manager decided to recognize a team of six for a quality improvement project which had yielded significant results in the department. Feeling well-informed on which team members had the most influence and had carried the greatest workload during the project, the decision was made to give three $100 cash awards and three $50 cash awards as a thank you to the team. Needless to say, the $100 recipients were thrilled and the $50 recipients were shocked, disappointed and demotivated. The team had worked together efficiently and effectively with dramatic results. But, this management error in judgment ensured that this team would probably never work together successfully again.

Unfortunately, the majority of current recognition systems rely upon the first-line manager's initiative and knowledge of recognition and motivation, as well as a thorough understanding of what is happening within their area of responsibility. Management is not trained, measured or compensated for their motivational skills, so this responsibility often falls to the wayside. Managers cannot be everywhere at once, so a huge number of opportunities for favorable notice and positive reinforcement are missed. So, in addition to changing the focus of leadership, all employees should be trained in recognition and positive reinforcement. By training all employees, we ensure that the actions and values we have deemed critical to our success are continuously and always reinforced. The "spirit" and pride that comes from feeling appreciated and knowing we are making a personal contribution to the success of the business returns, creating an atmosphere that encourages team play, goal achievement and innovation. By bringing our minds, hands AND hearts to the work equation, we are guaranteed better results in all of our endeavors.

LOWERING ATTRITION RATES

"For many of us, the most hopeful day on the job is our first."

One Size Fits One
Gary Heil, Tom Parker and Deborah C. Stephens

A study of 1000 executives from 150 of the largest companies in the United States conducted by Robert Half International revealed that 34% of employees cite the "lack of praise and recognition" as the number one reason they are leaving their jobs. In another report produced by Sunrise®, the authors state, *"During the last decade, both employer and employee loyalty have dropped dramatically, and with them employee interest and job quality. As the US economy shifts from a high-paying manufacturing base to a lower-paying service base, it is becoming harder to keep the excellent employees in vital positions."*

In the past decade, more and more companies have reduced their employee populations through RIFs (reduction in force), downsizing, or, for those who prefer the sugar-coated term, "right sizing." Employees know there is no such thing as employer loyalty in today's world. Hard work, long hours and loyalty do not guarantee job security any more. Due to this knowledge, people are busy making themselves marketable. They know how much their peers at other companies are making. They are continuously improving and updating their resumes.

What is this overturn costing us? Employee retention has become the most critical cost containment issue in American business. In ***Beyond Generation X,*** a book by Claire Raines, she shares several facts -

1) Employee retention is the top of the list of cost containment measures.

2) The *Wall Street Journal* has reported that it costs $2,900 - $10,000 to replace a shift manager.

3) Larry Forehand, president of the Texas Restaurant Association, reported on expensive labor replacement costs, as follows:

- Kitchen employee = $775
- Host = $658
- Server = $474
- Busser = $362

Forehand also reported that the average restaurant turnover rate is 200%, costing an average of $30,000 a year in employee replacement costs in restaurants.

These figures and the fact that your company's greatest new idea could walk out the front door to the competition at a moment's notice, make us realize that we need to create a new environment if we want to have exemplary employees working for us. More and more employees are demanding feedback and guidance about potential growth areas, as well as the environment and training required to improve their resumes and keep their skill set expanding.

In *One Size Fits One*, the authors provide a list of things to avoid in our personal work relationships: taking someone for granted, treating people as if they had no other options, not listening, not showing respect, not making employees feel important as people by demonstrating you genuinely care about them, and not treating employees as individuals. An effective recognition system addresses all of these items. In addition, the authors state, *"What we're looking for in our business relationships is companies and people who genuinely care as much about us as individuals as they do about their bottom-line and whose actions bear this out."*. There are common characteristics in our "loyal relationships"; we feel listened to, respected, cared for and special. An effective recognition system which provides the processes for showing appreciation and approval, and acknowledging each contribution to success, can help establish these loyal relationships.

Several companies have begun to realize that people are a company's most valuable asset. Regardless of your goals, programs and objectives, they are just a document until people bring them to reality. People are your competitive advantage. Jan Carlzon, former

CEO of Scandinavian Airlines stated, *"Equipment and real estate may be bought and sold, but the company with excellent employees enjoys the most priceless, hard-to-find, and sought-after asset."*

UNLEASHING THE UNTAPPED POTENTIAL OF OUR WORKFORCE

"Don't measure yourself by what you have accomplished, but by what you should have accomplished with your ability."

John Wooden
UCLA coach

Recently, a study was conducted by the Inventure Group in Eden Prairie, Minnesota. Five thousand people from a variety of organizations and industries were interviewed with the goal of discovering how connected people were to their jobs. The results showed that only 10 - 20% of employees are "engaged" in their work. The researchers defined "engaged" workers as employees that are productive, profess a high level of job satisfaction and are performing to their potential. On the other end of the spectrum (80 - 90%) were employees that were "burnt out" and "rusted out". Burnt out employees are those who are suffering from over-engagement, such as too much work or a feeling that nothing they contribute makes a difference. Although we have been bombarded by stories of work-related stress, this group represented a very small percentage. The largest part of the 80-90% consisted of "rusted out" employees described as using their time to avoid committing more than absolutely necessary to keep their jobs, doing the bare minimum to collect their paychecks and being disengaged. They are committed only to keeping the job, not to performing to their best abilities.

The Sunrise® Consulting Group, an independent consultant for the Lamont Corporation, collected information from several employer-employee relationship studies and shared the following items:

✓ Only 25% of employees work at full capability (this figure is slightly higher than the study by the Inventure Group).

✓   About 44% of employees exert only minimum effort.

Although the percentages do not exactly match on these reported results, both show that a sizable majority of our employees, 75-90% are not working to their full potential. Imagine for a moment what would happen if all of a sudden the entire workforce started working to their utmost best. Think what would happen if you could unlock this potential for your company. The entire culture would change to one of "state of the art" vs. standard, beyond expectation vs. just enough, creative display of skills and talents vs. rote performance of job tasks. Which culture would you prefer to work in? Which environment do you think would have the greatest impact on your bottom line?

People are our most valuable asset and thinking of how much more we could achieve if they were working at full potential makes us realize how we have underestimated their intelligence and talent. We have created robots, robbing our employees of the chance to make a difference. In *One Size Fits One*, it states

> *"The problem today is that it's a rare company, and an exceptional leader, who dares to devote the time and make the effort to form the human relationships with co-workers that lead to the commitment and to the unleashing of human potential we all say we're looking for . . . We must make unleashing the potential of people a strategic imperative."*

How can we establish the environment we need to unleash the untapped potential in our employees? Several actions will help to drive this new culture including:

✓   Recognize and reinforce each other for values we appreciate.

✓   Celebrate our team successes, goal achievement and any action of which we want to see more.

✓ Base our recognition and rewards on commitment, innovation, people skills and involvement vs. the old work ethic of obedience – doing what you're told, the way you're told to do it.

✓ Eliminate the corporate hierarchy and bureaucracy which undermines and demotivates our people.

✓ Ensure that your actions, policies and procedures ALL support the behaviors and practices necessary to reach your goals while demonstrating high values.

✓ Treat employees with the respect they deserve through immediate and constant appreciation, approval and acknowledgment.

✓ Provide the training.

✓ Set the example.

In *Beyond Generation X*, Claire Raines states, "Poorly treated employees perform poorly. Well-treated employees perform well." Many times, we have been asked, "How much will an effective recognition system cost us and what is the return on investment?" When you consider that the majority of your employees are not working up to their potential, the more important question would be, "How much is it costing you NOT to have an effective recognition system?

Assessing your recognition effectiveness

"You've got to be careful if you don't know where you're going, because you might not get there."

Yogi Berra

PRIOR to adopting a new recognition philosophy and implementing new tools and methods for positive reinforcement, it is important to establish a baseline. This baseline will provide you with valuable information that can be used to design your system and can be used in the future to determine whether or not your actions toward improving your recognition system and moving your organization toward business objectives have been effective.

This survey may be modified to fit your specific situation, however there are several features and methods of conducting the survey which will ensure the accuracy and integrity of the information. First, using a 1 to 7 scale will provide you with more discrimination, so that you may note any movement or shift in the data more quickly. You should ensure that, regardless of your selected sample size (initially, the larger, the better), you take steps to achieve an 100% response rate. This can be achieved by giving phone surveys, by conducting the survey in meetings where attendance is required, or, in the spirit of positive reinforcement, by offering some token of appreciation for participation.

Assessing your recognition effectiveness

Recognition Survey

Instructions: Please answer the following questions based on your personal recognition experiences in the last 12 months. Multiple responses to the same question are expected; choose as many as apply.

1. Did you receive recognition in the last 12 months? Yes ☐ No ☐

   If NO, proceed to Question 5?

   If YES, were you recognized as an individual or a team member?
   ☐ Individual ☐ Team member

2. Who recognized you?
   - ☐ Your manager
   - ☐ Another manager
   - ☐ Peer
   - ☐ Supplier
   - ☐ Customer
   - ☐ Other (please list) _____

3. Why were you recognized?
   - ☐ New idea/suggestion
   - ☐ Training/acquiring a new skill
   - ☐ Volunteer for special project
   - ☐ Cycle time reduction
   - ☐ Cost reduction
   - ☐ Quality improvement
   - ☐ Cultural contribution (i.e. community service, safety, work environment improvement, etc.)
   - ☐ Exemplifying a specific behavior or value (which value?) _____
   - ☐ Other (please list) _____

4. What method was used to recognize you?
   - ☐ One-on-one verbal recognition
   - ☐ Verbal, in front of a group
   - ☐ Thank you card
   - ☐ Special gift
   - ☐ Meal/special event (i.e. donuts, pizza, breakfast, lunch, dinner, baseball game, picnic, etc.) _____

Assessing your recognition effectiveness

❏ Other (please list)

5. To what degree do you consider recognition in your work group to be fair and consistent?

Recognition is consistent;   1   2   3   4   5   6   7   Seems to be for the chosen few;
I can depend on being   I do not feel I am appreciated
valued & appreciated.   when I put forth my best effort.

6. To what degree do you consider recognition in our work group to be meaningful?

I did not feel   1   2   3   4   5   6   7   Very meaningful;
appreciated   made me feel important

7. Did you initiate or give anyone recognition   Yes   No
in the last 12 months?   ❏   ❏

If NO, proceed to Question 11?

If YES, did you recognize an individual or a team/department?
❏ Individual   ❏ Team member

8. Who did you recognize?
❏ Your manager   ❏ Another manager
❏ Peer(s)   ❏ Supplier(s)
❏ Customer(s)   ❏ Other (please list) _____

9. Why did you recognize the individual/team?
❏ New idea/suggestion   ❏ Training/acquiring a new skill
❏ Volunteer for special project   ❏ Cycle time reduction
❏ Cost reduction   ❏ Quality improvement
❏ Cultural contribution (i.e. community service, safety, work
environment improvement, etc.)
❏ Exemplifying a core value (Which value?) _____
❏ Other (please list) _____

37

Assessing your recognition effectiveness

10. What method did you select?

☐ One-on-one verbal recognition ☐ Verbal, in front of a group

☐ Thank you card ☐ Special gift

☐ Meal/special event (i.e. donuts, pizza, breakfast, lunch, dinner, baseball game, picnic, etc.)

☐ Other (please list) _____

11. What type of non-cash recognition would you most appreciate?

☐ Time off ☐ Dining certificates

☐ Gift certificate for the local mall ☐ Logo gift

☐ Special event passes (movies, ball games, etc.)

☐ After hours celebration ☐ Non-logo gift

☐ Special work event (i.e. donuts, pizza, breakfast, lunch, dinner, picnic, party during work hours, etc.)

☐ Other (please list) _____

12. What suggestions do you have for improving the consistency of our recognition processes?

_____

_____

_____

_____

_____

_____

_____

_____

Question 1 helps you determine the percentage of your employee population being recognized on an annual basis. Your goal should be to recognize 100% of your employees as everyone should be making some positive contribution sometime during the course of the year. Everyone needs to feel noticed and appreciated. The second part of this question will reveal whether or not you equally value individual and team contributions. Business success is a combination of both types. Your recognition system should have provisions for both and one type should not have a higher perceived value than the other.

Question 2 will enable you to see who is driving the recognition. All of these relationships are critical to the business. Managers should be using positive reinforcement to drive performance to the highest level and to decrease the time it takes to achieve goals. Often, the recognition of a peer is the most valued, as they best understand the amount of knowledge, skills, time and labor required to accomplish specific tasks. Recognition from a supplier indicates that the employee is striving to build the "give and take" relationship that will best serve the company's interest. Recognition from another manager demonstrates that the employee is flexible and possibly working to build those interdepartmental and interfunctional relationships that benefit the business. Of course, the highest form of recognition comes from the customer. When an employee is recognized by a customer, it is a positive reflection on your company's product/service. All of these sources of recognition are important, as they represent different relationships and the associated valued behaviors/practices. All of these relationships are critical to maximizing performance.

Question 3 will show you at a glance what practice is the most valued in the work group you are interviewing. You can determine if your recognition system is reinforcing what you have deemed to be the most critical to the success of the business.

Question 4 provides information on employee preferences and the list makes employees aware of all of the current available options. You can enhance this part of the survey by adding your own specific recognition tools and awards.

Question 5 information may be displayed on a control chart. It is very important that business and performance requirements are directly tied to recognition, and that these requirements are communicated and documented to ensure consistency. In addition, making recognition the responsibility of every person helps eliminate the common complaints of management favoritism.

Question 6 information also may be placed on a control chart, enabling the user to monitor recognition over time. If recognition is not perceived as meaningful, then it is NOT positive reinforcement.

Questions 7 through 11 ask the same questions from the perspective of the giver. These questions reinforce that recognition is the responsibility of everyone.

Question 12 allows for comments and suggestions. In addition, if you are responsible for creating a new recognition system, you will want to address the following questions:

✓ What behaviors or values are critical to our business success?

✓ What goals do we wish to achieve quickly and effectively?

✓ Have we translated these goals into the required individual/team short-term actions, so that we may recognize progress?

✓ Do we have methods in place to celebrate milestones and goal achievement? Are there methods for individual, team, department and company milestones?

✓ Do we have tools to recognize both individuals and teams?

✓ Should we require measurable results?

✓ What celebration opportunities do we expect for our company in the next year?

✓ How can we make our recognition tools readily available and easy to get while maintaining control?

Collecting the information from the survey and answering the previous questions will help you determine what you need to do. This book will provide you with some valuable definitions, lessons learned, proven tools and suggested delivery methods that will help you be successful in designing customizing and implementing your system.

Section 1:

MEANING

*The deepest principle in human nature is the craving to be **appreciated**.*
William James

*I have yet to find the person, however great or exalted his station, who did not do better work and put forth greater effort under a spirit of **approval**, than he would ever do under a spirit of criticism*
Charles Schwab

*You have to catch people in the act of doing a good job and **acknowledge** them individually and specifically for a job well done*
Kathryn Wall
Recognition Secrets Seminar

What recognition really means

"The capacity for delight is the gift of paying attention."

Julia Cameron

THE *Random House College Dictionary* defines recognition as:

1. The act of recognizing someone or something.

2. The state of being recognized.

3. The perception or *acknowledgment* of something as true or valid.

4. *Appreciation* of achievements, merit, services, etc., or an expression of this.

5. Formal acknowledgment conveying *approval.*

The definition is easy to remember by focusing on the three A's – acknowledgment, appreciation and approval. Effective recognition will always include all three. One example of a company recognition statement that embodies the three A's is:

"To *acknowledge* and *appreciate* those behaviors, practices and actions that move us toward achieving our business goals and objectives, and that establish a working environment that promotes the values and concepts of loyalty, belonging, confidence, self-worth, teamwork, respect, creativity and trust through frequent and sincere methods of *approval*."

There are several methods, tools, gifts and awards available for recognition. Regardless of which you prefer or select, the recognition must incorporate seven basic characteristics to be effective – it must be sincere, fair and consistent, timely, frequent, flexible, appropriate and specific.

Sincere

"Our actions speak louder than words; leadership style is important and it communicates who we really are. When we try a style that is not us, that we don't believe in, we fool no one."

One Size Fits All
Gary Heil, Tom Parker & Deborah C. Stephens

There is absolute truth in the old adage, *"It's not the gift, it's the thought that counts."* Heartfelt, warm and sincere appreciation is what drives performance in a positive direction. The person receiving the recognition must FEEL valued to realize the benefits of positive reinforcement – repeated behaviors and peak performance. Let's look at two different service award processes:

This week marks Jim's 20-year anniversary with his company. On Monday, he receives a large envelope in his interoffice mail. He opens it. On top is a form letter from his CEO, congratulating him on all his hard work. Jim laughs and thinks to himself, "The CEO doesn't even know my name, let alone what I do here." He looks at the rest of the package. A catalog is enclosed containing ten items, none of which Jim is remotely interested in. He decides to select one to give as a Christmas present to his aunt. Then, he dials the "1-800" number. The computerized telephone message says, "You have reached the 'Lazy Boss Awards Company'. Please enter your company number located on the front of the catalog." Jim enters the number. "John Doe, Incorporated," the computer voice announces after a few moments, "Enter your employee number." Jim enters his employee number. "Congratulations . . . (long pause while the computer looks up the employee number), Jim. Please enter your gift selection number." Jim enters the number of the gift he does not want. "Thank you!" the computer voice concludes and the "conversation" is over. Six to eight weeks later, Jim receives his anniversary present. Does he FEEL appreciated and valued? No. Has he been motivated to new levels of performance? No. Would your CEO even dream of trying this anniversary approach on his/her spouse – not personally calling, waiting to celebrate for five years and delivering the gift six to eight weeks later? I don't think so. This practice is not personal or sincere.

Today is Tim's 17th anniversary. At the beginning of the year, his manager created a list of his employees and their anniversary dates from his employee records. He has marked each one in his calendar. When Tim walks into his office, there is a "Happy Anniversary" balloon and a cupcake with a candle in it. The manager walks in shortly after Tim and says, "Happy Anniversary, Tim. You've had quite a year, this year. I will never forget how you came to the rescue when I forgot those financial figures I needed at the off-site. You dropped everything and rushed to help me. I really can't imagine what this office would be like without you. Thanks, Tim, for everything!" Later, Tim's manager takes his picture with his co-workers and they present him with a journal. Each of his co-workers has signed the book and written down a special memory from the last year that included Tim or a special quality Tim has that they appreciate. Will Tim remember this anniversary? Yes. He has a picture, a journal and a "memory". Will his manager benefit? You bet! He showed sincere appreciation and focused on the "thought". Tim feels like his manager cares and will reciprocate many times during the next year. And, what was the cost of giving this annual service award? $14. What was the value to the company? Priceless.

I once heard a presentation that promised ten years of data on how to motivate employees. The consultant, who charged $5K, shared that people will do anything for a TV, as they chose electronics more than any other award out of their catalogs. I might choose a TV, if offered, but that is no guarantee that my performance will improve or that I truly FEEL appreciated. The mitigating factors are how the gift was given to me and how I feel. Be SINCERE.

FAIR AND CONSISTENT

"I believe that if you create an environment that your people identify with, that is responsive to their sense of values, justice, fairness, ethics, compassion, and appreciation, they will help you be successful."

Robert Haas
CEO - Levi Strauss

Recognition loses its power and value if it is perceived as inequitable and inconsistently applied. Carla O'Dell, author of **People, Performance and Pay**, has compiled survey results that reveal that the majority of current recognition systems in the US are management driven and that recognition results from such subjective means as management nomination, supervisory commendations, etc. Further, out of 271 companies surveyed, the mean percentage of the employee population recognized on an annual basis was less than 5%. Not a very good average, considering everyone has an innate need to feel noticed and appreciated. Often, only the "squeaky wheel gets the grease".

Every person in the workplace makes a contribution. Every person has room for improvement. Every person should have an equal opportunity for recognition. In order for us to be successful, now and in the future, we need to tap into each individual's potential

What recognition really means

and talents. We need more than 5% of our employees working toward our success. To accomplish this, we must define and establish recognition criteria for every employee, and set a goal of recognizing 100% of our workforce.

Losers Manufacturing Company started a new suggestion system. Employees who submitted any idea during the last year received an invitation to a big formal banquet at a fancy hotel. Each special guest expects to receive some type of award at the banquet for their specific contribution to the success of the business. Tracy, a single mom living from pay day to pay day, has seen her suggestion implemented and her organization benefit to the tune of $300,000 per year. She is excited to be able to realize her award finally. Tracy buys a new dress, hires a babysitter and finds a date. "Never mind the expense!" she thinks. "I am going to get my award." She goes to the banquet, beaming with pride. Upon arriving, she receives a ticket stub with a serial number. "They are having a drawing, too. How nice!" she thinks. Dinner is served. Two of the executives give speeches on how important innovation is to the future of their business. Finally, one of them announces: "It's time to give out the awards!" Two hundred people move to the edge of their seats, excitedly awaiting announcement of their name and achievement. Then, the barrel with the tickets is moved on to the stage. Five people out of the 200 receive a prize. The grand prize-winner receives a trip for two to the Caribbean for her suggestion to put an aloe vera plant next to a soldering iron. The other 195 never hear their name or accomplishment announced, and go home with a coffee mug commemorating this "momentous" nightmare. Tracy goes home with a $3 coffee mug that all the "losers" received and tears in her eyes. There are 195 people who will not submit another idea; this suggestion system has demotivated more people than it has motivated. One has to wonder how much money the company lost in new ideas the next year from this unfair and inconsistent process.

What recognition really means

A restaurant owner wants to increase his sales. He thinks sales would increase if his wait staff would offer (suggestive sell) appetizers when taking drink orders. He brings the group together and asks them to begin offering appetizers prior to taking dinner orders at every table. At the end of the week, he notices that there has been no increase in sales. "Of course!" he thinks, "I forgot the positive reinforcement." The owner knows that the most valuable, non-monetary award he can offer his wait staff is paid time off. So, he brings the group together again and asks them to suggest appetizers, but this time he adds: "For every ten appetizers sold, the waiter or waitress will receive one hour paid time off." Each wait person has the ability and opportunity to realize this reinforcement, making this system fair. Each table's check includes the name of the wait person, making it a very trackable system which can be consistently applied. This story has a happy ending – the restaurant owner realized a 30% rise in sales.

In *Bringing Out the Best in People*, Aubrey Daniels discusses the values that need to be inculcated in your approach to managing people. One of these values is "justice." Daniels defines justice as "each person getting what he/she deserves". Further he adds: "Those who perform well will get more reinforcement than those who perform poorly". You must set performance objectives for your business, translate these into individual behaviors and actions, and reinforce each person accordingly for his/her contribution toward achieving the objective. Every person has some value or skill that he/she can apply toward the success of the organization or business. BE FAIR AND CONSISTENT.

Timely

"Just as the accumulation of small improvements can make a dramatic, lasting change in the organization's products or services, the repeated numerous small occasions of taking note of the contributions of individuals and teams can create a different company."

Patrick Townsend and Joan Gebhardt
The Quality Process: Little Things Mean A Lot

Anyone who has taken Psychology 101 knows that *the more immediate the recognition, the more likely the behavior will be repeated*. Immediate recognition is critical for the following reasons:

- The noteworthy act is still clear in the minds of the giver and receiver.
- You don't accidentally forget to recognize by waiting for an occasion.
- The recognition is more meaningful.
- Recognition is more likely to be remembered and the behavior/practice is more likely to be repeated.
- There is more emotion and feeling the closer the recognition is to the occurrence.

If you want to give a celebration, a special gift or a token of appreciation later, you must ensure that the praise and sincere thanks are given immediately.

Ted's manager rolls up performance metrics quarterly. The first ten weeks of the quarter, Ted has consistently produced the largest number of invoices with the least amount of errors per week. But, the last two weeks of the quarter, Ted must go out of state due to a death in his family. Ted's manager rolls up the quarterly report and it shows that Steve has processed the most invoices for the quarter. Of course, Steve has an accuracy problem, but all the report shows is "the most". Two weeks after the end of the quarter, Ted returns just in time to see Steve receive a new watch for his outstanding productivity. No favorable attention is given to Ted. This recognition was not timely, leaves Steve thinking he is doing the best and Ted thinking "Why do I even try?"

Seymour Good manages a customer complaints department. He knows that the bottom line is directly impacted by how well his workers resolve complaints. Ned receives a call and the customer is beyond irate. Ned handles the situation with unusual poise and finesse, sending someone to the customer's home within the hour to fix the problem. Later, he calls the customer back to ensure that he is satisfied with the solution. The customer is so impressed with Ned's concern that he calls back and talks to the department manager, complimenting Ned and the wonderful service he received. Ned and his son are big baseball fans, so Seymour Good immediately gets on the phone and orders tickets for the game scheduled the next day in the afternoon. He goes to Ned and shares how happy he is with the customer compliment and that he knows Ned has been working really hard to increase customer satisfaction. Then, he says, "I have two tickets for tomorrow's baseball game at 'will call' for you. Hopefully, your son will be able to join you. I'd like to give you the tickets and the time off to attend to show you just how much I appreciate the way you handled this customer." Ned is thrilled and he gets to share his excitement and his accomplishment with his family. This recognition is timely and Ned returns to work ready to handle whatever comes his way.

Recognition must be as immediate as possible. The impact of the recognition reduces as time goes by. Many experts believe that if you have waited a week, it is too long and you have sacrificed any chance you had of increasing the positive behavior. In addition, you run the risk of reinforcing the wrong behavior, as in the case of Ted and Steve. Plan and BE TIMELY.

Frequent

"To keep a lamp burning, we have to keep putting oil on it."

Mother Teresa

Saying thanks and showing appreciation should be a daily activity at a minimum. Saying "thank you" and recognizing employees are not great investments and should be applied liberally! The benefits from frequent, sincere appreciation can positively impact every bottom-line measurement – productivity, sales, product and service quality, customer satisfaction, employee attrition, and so forth. Recognition should be a habit and part of every employee's training. Every manager should become a role model, exemplifying the principles required to establish mutually satisfying and beneficial work relationships.

So often, corporate recognition programs are created with only "administrative-ease" in mind. Providing everyone with a Thanksgiving or Christmas turkey is a nice gesture, but it is NOT recognition. It takes a minimum of planning and execution (4000 employees = 4000 turkeys; order in October). A nice form letter complete with the CEO's stamped signature usually accompanies the gift, thanking the employee for the past year of service. What are some of the messages this form of so-called recognition sends?

"Yippee! If I can stick it out in this thankless job another year, I can get another turkey!"

"Gee, my co-worker was undependable and did low quality work and he/she gets the same thanks I do!"

"If it wasn't a holiday, they probably wouldn't thank me at all!"

"Thanks for another year of service? You don't even know my name!"

This method does not feel like sincere appreciation. It does not reinforce any specific behavior or practice unless it is meant to recognize just being in the workplace at some time, doing something, somewhere, somehow during the last year. And, recognizing once annually is just not enough.

There is a manufacturing department that is trying to build the first lot of a new product. Due to the many quality and process problems typical of a new product, they have fallen behind schedule. The manager looks at the schedule for the quarter; her group will have to produce 12 widgets a day vs. the 10 widgets they produced on their very best day so far. She calls together the department and shares: "As you all know, we have fallen behind schedule and might miss our customer commitments due to the quality and process problems we've encountered. We need to produce twelve widgets a day to get back on track. Here is my plan. #1 - We will have to work overtime on any day we don't produce twelve widgets. #2 - I am going to put this bell at the end of the line. Any Monday through Thursday that we produce twelve widgets and get them past inspection and test before the end of the normal shift, I want you to ring the bell and go to the break area. I am buying snacks and sodas. We will stay in the break area the rest of the shift and try to figure out those quality and process problems. #3 - I have placed a siren at the end of the line, too. As soon as you produce the twelve widgets successfully before the end of the normal shift on Friday, you may 'blow the siren' and go home to start your weekend early. #4 - If we successfully complete this quarter and make our customer commitments, I am going to bring in my barbecue grill and personally cook your lunch. I'll even wear my chef's hat and apron. Let's do it!"

The first week went as follows:

- ✓ Monday - one hour overtime
- ✓ Tuesday - one hour overtime

What recognition really means

- ✓ Wednesday - thirty minutes overtime
- ✓ Thursday - thirty minutes prior to shift end; the bell rings, the manager buys soda and snacks and the group brainstorms 20 different process and quality problems.
- ✓ Friday - work successfully completed one hour prior to shift end; the siren blows.

The second week, they begin consistently completing their work early. They spend this time prioritizing the problems and beginning to work on resolutions. Friday, the siren blows again. Needless to say, they end the quarter on schedule, the problem list is cut from 20 to two, and the manager is barbecuing lunch. The team has pulled together; individuals automatically moved to the critical path in their process and functioned as true teammates. The process has improved dramatically. Customer orders have been met. The manager frequently reinforced her group, every step along the way.

The group is now able to easily produce the nine widgets a day required to keep the current schedule, so in the spirit of continuous improvement, the manager has decided to work on cross-training for the next few weeks. Her recognition plan includes 15 minutes off for each of the 20 stations you learn and a big graduation cake and ceremony with "diplomas" when everyone is trained.

The more frequently you recognize behaviors, actions and practices, the more often you will see them. Take your goals and break them into small milestones which will provide you opportunities to reinforce progress. When possible, do this not only for your team, but for each individual's performance. You will reach your goals more quickly than before, which more than compensates for your planning and administrative time. BE FREQUENT.

FLEXIBLE

"In every individual interaction you have, you have some awesome choices, and only you can decide whether they will be positive or negative."

Barbara Glanz
Care Packages for the Workplace

In the 90s, there has been a major focus on cultural diversity. When designing a recognition system, it is critical to understand not only cultural differences, but individual differences. You must approach each recognition act with the knowledge that *every single person is different and unique*. One size does not fit all; the one or two tools that most companies provide for recognition will never do the trick.

Mary's department has been struggling for the last month to manufacture a new toy for the Christmas shopping rush. Their manager has promised them a "big surprise" if they successfully make their deadline. They just barely make it – ten minutes to spare. The manager comes to give them their recognition. "I have arranged for our entire group to have a steak dinner with our CEO at the fanciest restaurant in town." Mary, a vegetarian, is not pleased with the menu. In addition, she is very uncomfortable about having dinner conversation with the CEO, who she doesn't know from Adam. She doesn't know what to wear. This "recognition" has become a nightmare for Mary – more like abuse than appreciation.

Seymour Good has just been appointed General Manager at a new subsidiary. He wants to meet more of the workers to acquaint them with his leadership style, which is really quite different from the previous GM's. The company has a peer-to-peer token system for thanking each other. The tokens are silver. Good decides to get himself an exact replica of the token in gold. When the workers go to get a token for a co-worker, they must reach into a brown bag to get the token. If they pull out the "golden token," the person they are thanking gets Good's services for two hours. Of course, their request must be legal, ethical and moral. The first year, Good washes someone's car in the parking lot, babysits while a worker goes grocery shopping, takes an employee and three friends for happy hour after work serving as designated driver, and answers the phones for a secretary. Everyone at the plant either hears the stories or witnesses the GM in his recognition activities. Good has established himself as a person who cares about his employees and who never says, "I can't." In turn, his employees have begun to reflect this attitude.

Each person is special in their own way. Make sure that your recognition system allows you to be flexible and make the reinforcement a positive experience. One person's positive experience may be very negative to another person. Use different "strokes" for different folks. Recognition is a very personal and emotional matter, making it critical to ensure enough flexibility to meet the recipient's needs. BE FLEXIBLE.

APPROPRIATE

"When people are afforded the opportunity to focus freely on their work, and that opportunity is backed by high expectations and appropriate rewards, they'll – guess what? – do their jobs."

Bill Catlette and Richard Hadden
Contented Cows Give Better Milk

The recognition method selected should match the level of effort expended, the behavior exemplified or the results achieved. You must provide a thoughtful structure that ensures the right recognition accompanies the right situation and the right person.

Tom is a development engineer who has been spending nights and weekends getting a product ready for market in October.

His boss, realizing this has been a long, tedious haul that will not end for another three months, orders Tom a dozen golf balls with the company logo. Tom, who doesn't own a set of golf clubs, let alone like golf, receives the gift and thinks "Even if I liked golf, there wouldn't be any time until the dead of winter." Tom puts the golf balls in the back of his bottom desk drawer.

Happy day! Tom, our development engineer, gets a new boss due to a corporate restructuring. His new boss notices a picture of Tom's wife and children on his desk and says: "They really must miss you when you're putting in this many hours." Tom replies, "Yeah, but not half as much as I miss them." That day, Tom's boss has flowers delivered to Tom's wife thanking her for sharing Tom during this critical stage of the development process. Then, Tom's boss gives him a dinner certificate and movie tickets and says: "Go home on time tonight, Tom. That is an order. Treat your family to dinner and a movie. You have been working so hard and I really appreciate your dedication. I am confident that we will make the schedule and I think a little break for you isn't going to make or break us. In fact, you might find it energizing." Tom feels noticed and appreciated. He sees his boss values the importance of family in his life. Tom will get the project completed on schedule.

What you value is not necessarily what is important to your employee. You must take the time to know the person and find out what he/she values. The recognition should match the specific situation. BE APPROPRIATE.

Specific

"Instead of passing judgment on what's right and wrong, good and bad, acceptable and unacceptable, successful managers value the unique contributions of each of their people."

Claire Raines
Beyond Generation X

Recipients should know exactly what they are being thanked for. The whole premise of recognition is that you want a specific behavior or practice to be repeated (performance improvement).

Linda works as a meeting planner for her company. This week she has organized three big events – an executive golf tournament, a sales seminar and a formal dinner/dance to appreciate customers. Her boss leaves a note from the CEO that says "Thanks. It was the greatest ever!" What was the greatest ever - the golf tournament, the class or the dinner dance? What behavior or activity should Linda repeat? This was a nice gesture, but, because it wasn't specific, there is no behavior reinforced.

Lucy is always punctual; her work assignments are consistently completed ahead of schedule. Although Lucy will never get a patent or save the company a million dollars, her boss really appreciates her dependability. He comes to work very early the next morning and places an engraved clock on Lucy's desk that says "Thanks for your impeccable timing!" The gift matches the contribution. Every time Lucy looks at her desk clock, she remembers she has been noticed and she is appreciated.

If you want to improve performance and ensure that good behaviors and practices are continued, you must call special attention to the action or behavior you appreciate. BE SPECIFIC.

Acknowledgment, appreciation and approval are all required to qualify an action as "recognition". In addition, you must ensure that all seven characteristics of effective recognition are covered when designing or selecting a method or tool. For example, a form letter is an acknowledgment, but lacks sincerity or a personal demonstration of approval for a specific individual's behavior, action or practice. Holiday turkeys or service awards given every five years acknowledge an employee's presence, but not much more. The missing ingredient in these recipes is what makes individuals want to change, be their best and come to work - "heart."

"To handle yourself,
Use your head;
To handle others,
Use your heart."

Author Unknown

Recognition and reward are not synonomous!

"It's easy to make a buck. It's a lot tougher to make a difference."

Tom Brokaw

"What's the use you learning to do right, when it's troublesome to do right and ain't no trouble to do wrong, and the wages is just the same?"

Mark Twain
The Adventures of Huckleberry Finn

RECOGNITION and reward are often used synonymously or are combined in a title of one system – the R & R system. These terms are very different and often the efforts to improve R & R systems totally neglect recognition. It is critical to clearly define these terms or you may fail to meet the performance improvement, employee satisfaction measures and quality of work life you are intending to attain.

As defined previously, recognition is *acknowledgment, appreciation and approval*. These elements, when combined and applied appropriately produce a psychological benefit – individuals have a sense of belonging and are motivated. *Webster's New Collegiate Dictionary* (G. & C. Merriam Co., 1981) defines reward in the following ways:

1. To give a reward to or for.

2. Recompense.

3. Something that is given in return for good or evil done or received and especially that is offered or given for a service.

Reward clearly indicates a financial benefit. Nothing in the definition indicates a psychological benefit. In fact, the definition reveals, as does history, that rewards can be gained for evil, as well as good.

A survey and report by Carla O'Dell and Jerry McAdams, published by the American Compensation Association revealed the following insights:

✓ A high 90.9% of respondents ranked "recognition when I've done a job well" as Important or Very Important as a motivational factor. Surprisingly, it ranked above "competitive salary" and "pay clearly tied to performance" (rewards).

✓ Only 54.4% reported that their workplace provided this recognition.

✓ The median budget for recognition was $7 - $23 per employee per year.

✓ Only 4 - 5% of the people in the companies surveyed received recognition on an annual basis. This is due to the fact that the recognition is set up for the employee of the month, salesperson of the year, best service team, etc. These programs severely limit the number of people who qualify for recognition.

✓ 75% of the respondents indicated subjective criteria, such as "management discretion," "supervisory nomination," and "superior performance event," and these were used to justify the decision to recognize.

Several conclusions can be drawn from these surveys. People want to be appreciated. Present work systems are not addressing this need. Receiving recognition is for the "chosen few" versus the "vital many" (everyone needs recognition). Most systems are subjective, competitive, demotivating to the majority who are losers, and are management-driven.

W. Edwards Deming once stated: *"People are born with a need for relationships with other people, and with the need to be loved and esteemed by others. There is innate need for self-esteem and respect. Management that denies to their employees dignity and self-esteem will smother intrinsic motivation."* Self-esteem, respect, intrinsic motivation and dignity are not guaranteed by a competitive salary.

Should recognition include a cash reward? In **People, Performance and Pay** by Carla O'Dell in collaboration with Jerry McAdams, a summary of data collected on non-monetary awards versus cash rewards showed there was approximately a 13% performance improvement using either non-monetary or cash awards. The cost of cash was nearly 12 cents for every dollar of increase. The cost of non-monetary awards was 4.1 cents for every dollar. Non-monetary awards clearly show a "significantly better return on investment". There is also a conclusion that in many situations, non-monetary awards are more suitable than cash.

Of course, reward or compensation is very important, but having a very competitive compensation package does not eliminate the need for focus on recognition. The only way to ensure the appropriate level of concentration on recognition is to totally separate it from reward. Let's look at the differences:

Recognition and reward are not synonomous!

Recognition	Reward
Non-cash	Monetary
Needed frequently	Infrequent changes
Psychological	Financial
Reinforces behaviors that can change corporate culture and practices permanently; facilitates long-term changes	Supports short-term objectives; usually set up on an annual cycle.
Personal - from the "heart"	Impersonal - "from the bank"
Value and principle based	Based on corporate budget
Used to keep employees	Used to attract employees

The amount of time we invest in the workplace and our need to have positive interactions with others demand that recognition moves to the forefront of our work priorities. It can dramatically improve the quality of our work life. How often do we need to hear "Another day, another dollar," or "I'm only here for the paycheck," before we go to work with our elaborate problem-solving processes to identify the root cause for this attitude? How many stress-related illnesses will we endure before we make creation of a good work environment a strategic priority by allowing people to care about each other and celebrate successes?

Just understanding the differences between reward and recognition may seem like a monumental task. There are some very simple solutions to this "recognition vs. reward" dilemma:

1) Never use recognition and reward in the same sentence.

2) Never have recognition and reward facilitated or administered by the same person, team or functional

62

group. Recognition requires people with psychological and motivational experience and expertise, while reward requires someone with financial, accounting and legal knowledge.

3) Keep cash for compensation; create a focus of sincere appreciation for recognition, and if combined with a tangible, make it a non-monetary award.

4) Train everyone in the importance of giving and receiving feedback in the workplace; do not limit this to a management responsibility.

5) Never give recognition based on a competition, lottery or subjective judgment; identify and recognize all efforts that contribute to meeting your business vision, goals and objectives.

6) In order for recognition to be meaningful and function as positive reinforcement, it must come from someone who knows the recipient personally and knows what they value. There should never be a corporate strategy or corporate strategic team for recognition. Give your first line the resources and training; provide a tool box, but don't ever limit recognition to just those tools. Allow those recognizing to be personal and creative.

Positive reinforcement
- the scientific evidence

"You never know what little bundle of encouragements artists carry around with them, what little pats on the back from what hands, what newspaper clipping, what word of hope from what teacher. I suppose the so-called faith in ourselves is the foundation of our talent, but I am sure the encouragements are the mortar that holds it together."

Luciano Pavrotti
Quoted in *My Friend Pavarotti* by Candido Bonvicini

AS mentioned previously, behavioral scientists have been studying the effect of positive reinforcement for more than 80 years and the results have been proven time and time again. We attempt to use positive reinforcement in the workplace by designing recognition systems and implementing incentive programs. Our desires are to achieve goals more quickly and to drive change effectively, but often our attempts fail as we have not applied the proven scientific principles.

<u>Principle #1 – A positive reinforcer is any stimulus that when present, changes or increases a behavior.</u>

Positive reinforcers can range from the very subtle – a smile, a nod, paying attention (changing the lighting/Hawthorne effect), providing training, increasing responsibility, to the obvious – awards and commendations that workers know they must "do this" to "get this". There are many instances in the workplace when we are reinforced for the wrong things. For example, numbers over quality or sales over honesty. These are not good long-term strategies for the business that wants to stay in business. It is not that the leaders in these examples want their employees to sacrifice quality or honesty, but they are positively reinforcing the "numbers" at these specific times and they are getting exactly what they are reinforcing. Aubrey Daniels states in **Bringing Out the Best in People**, *"People do what they do because of what happens to them when they do it"*. So, when things are not operating the way you planned or desired, you must look at what is presently being reinforced, stop reinforcing the wrong thing and create a method to positively reinforce the desired behavior, action or practice.

Principle #2 – Reinforcers vary in their quality.

Different forms of positive reinforcement have different degrees of impact on each individual. While simply paying attention may drive a 5% improvement, buying a lunch may yield 10% or giving the individual a paid day off may yield a 25% improvement. Recognition is a very personal matter, often requiring several trials. It requires really knowing the person and what they value the most.

Principle #3 – The immediacy of delivery of a reinforcer determines how effective it is.

The whole purpose of using positive reinforcement is to introduce a new behavior or increase a behavior. There must be a direct link between the action and the reinforcement. Although there is a slight difference in time estimations, the majority of scientific studies agree that the positive reinforcement has virtually lost all possible impact after seven to fourteen days. The more immediate the recognition, the more likely you are to see the behavior repeated.

Most performance evaluation systems, profit sharing plans and recognition processes are set up on annual cycles (at best, quarterly cycles) rendering them ineffective at driving performance improvement or tapping into the discretionary effort of our employees. This is why it is critical to establish a recognition system that provides tools and methods that may be used immediately after the act or accomplishment you have identified as a performance worth repeating.

Principle #4 – A reinforcer can be effective for one person, but not for another.

Recognition is a very personal matter that requires "different strokes for different folks". *One size fits all systems* are doomed to fail as reinforcement. Some employees appreciate overtime, others place a high value on their time off. Some employees like public attention, others prefer their praise in private. Some like ball caps and some collect coffee mugs. You will never find one method that suits everyone. To be effective, you must personally know the person you are recognizing.

Principle #5 – The same reinforcer can be effective at one time, but ineffective at another.

As always, timing is everything. A day off might be very effective as recognition at the end of an engineering project, but in the middle of a development cycle, when there are deadlines and days off mean getting further behind, it may be perceived as negative. If a manager gives a pizza party or brings doughnuts every week, employees come to expect it and lose interest, making the recognition ineffective. The key is to have a variety of methods and to present the right recognition at the right time.

Principle #6 – Reinforcers vary in their intensity.

How long does the impact of the positive reinforcement last? About ten years ago, I received $100 for an outstanding accomplishment. I don't remember how I spent the $100; knowing where I was at that point in time, I probably paid a late bill. The accomplishment, I believe, had to do with rewriting a procedure. What procedure? I am not sure. This recognition experience was not memorable or intense. Two years ago, I was asked to plan a baseball game for 1000 people. This is not a normal task for an engineer to undertake. A friend of mine at work had passed away a month earlier and the game was to be dedicated to him. I wrote the script to be flashed on the scoreboard in his memory. A manager took a snapshot of the scoreboard with the message, enlarged the photo and framed it. He presented it to me with his thanks for organizing the event. I have been asked to do several "out of the ordinary" things for this manager since this event. This recognition was intense for me. And, what behaviors were reinforced? Accepting new challenges and working outside of my job description to meet a unique need are now my normal operating habits.

Principle #7 – What administrators expect to function as reinforcers often do not correspond to what their recipients actually find to be reinforcing.

This fact is obvious given that 54% of survey recipients from over 271 companies who responded that their companies did not provide them with any recognition for a job well done. I am sure these companies have service award programs and performance evaluation systems, and most of them have profit sharing, yet still the respondents feel their efforts go unnoticed and unrecognized. Also, we often select what we would like to receive if we were the recipient, which is exactly what the employees would not like.

Principle #8 – Reinforcing progress always improves performance more dramatically than reinforcing results.

All of our compensation systems, as well as the majority of recognition systems, are based on long-term results. We give our employees annual goals and sit back a year to wait to see if they achieve them. There are several things wrong with this approach.

✓   *The employee might be able to achieve the goal in less time.*
     Wouldn't this be to a company's benefit? Deadlines
     give us permission to procrastinate.

Positive reinforcement - the scientific evidence

✓ *Why do more work for the same money?*
If my goal is to reduce my cycle time by one hour and I can do this in one month, I am obviously going to be doing more work for the same pay for 11 months. Why stress myself?

✓ *The difference between an average performer and an outstanding performer equates to between one and two percent of pay raise.*
Again, why strain myself? On the other hand, we can't be giving raises and going through the corporate bureaucracy every week. The trick is to set meaningful, visible (have a measurement the employee can see) and short-term goals, AND immediately recognize these milestones. It is important that you don't automatically increase the goal and the work load (this is negative reinforcement). Gently guide your people toward the objective using recognition. For example, Andy increases the number of invoices he processes from eight to ten in four weeks. His manager's objective is to get each person's total to 12 by the end of the year. When Andy reaches ten, his boss says, "Andy, I don't know how you did it! You must be cross-eyed from filling in all those numbers, so I got you this poster for your office. I know you enjoy golf – it's a picture of Pebble Beach. I thought maybe when you're resting your eyes, you could rest them on this beauty. Tell me, how did you do it?" Andy, having been given "bragging rights" by his boss, shares his success story. His boss replies: "That was really a clever approach. Whenever you complete ten invoices, I want you to look at Pebble Beach and just spend the rest of the day dreaming up some other ideas to simplify the process. Make sure you write them down, so you don't forget them."

Andy has been shown that increased invoices mean recognition and that his ideas are important. By the end of the year, his invoice rate is 16 due to implementation of some of his simplification ideas he gained on his "trips" to Pebble Beach. Every time a person makes a noticeable performance improvement, managers need to be on hand with recognition to reinforce progress (the small wins). You will see amazing results without waiting a year.

Principle #9 – Positive reinforcement is always more effective than negative reinforcement, extinction and punishment.

Look at your corporate policies and procedures. Hundreds of pages of negative consequences for everything from parking in the wrong space to insider trading. Now, look for the positive reinforcement section. What? It's not there? Two things to remember: #1 – Positive reinforcement is the only way to drive people to their highest level of performance and #2 – No one has ever been punished into their best performance. As the next chapter indicates, we do need to have negative consequences in our repertoire, but the concentration should be on tapping into that great untapped resource – the talent and potential of our people.

The flip side -
negative reinforcement and
negative consequences

"There are two great motivators in life. One is fear. The other is love. You can manage by fear, but if you do you will ensure that people don't perform up to their real capabilities.
But, if you manage people by love – that is, if you show them respect and trust – they perform up to their real capabilities."

Jan Carlzon
Moments of Truth

TRY to recall your classes or pick up a textbook used for Psychology 101. When you reference "reinforcement", you will most likely find the term "behaviorism". Behaviorism is very simply the study of behavior and the scientists who developed this particular school of thought proved with their experiments that ALL learning and behavior changes occur through reinforcement. You can understand what is happening with an individual, team or workforce by associating the positive or negative consequences in their environment that follow specific behaviors.

The previous chapter discussed positive reinforcement in detail. Other forms of reinforcement include negative reinforcement, punishment and extinction. Definitions of these forms of recognition from a textbook entitled *Understanding Motivation and Emotion* are:

✓ **Negative reinforcement**
Any stimulus that, when removed, INCREASES the probability of behavior.

✓ **Punishers**
Any stimulus that, when present, DECREASES the probability of a behavior.

✓ **Extinction**
Discontinuation of a stimulus that previously reinforced a behavior; DECREASES a behavior.

It is important to note that these are the reinforcers most used in the workplace and not one of these three methods of reinforcement taps into the discretionary efforts of people. If you are trying to achieve an atmosphere of innovation, creativity and high productivity, you cannot negatively reinforce, punish or ignore a person into these higher levels of performance.

Negative reinforcement, like positive reinforcement, increases behavior, however it is different than positive reinforcement in that it produces only enough performance change to escape or avoid an aversive consequence. Aubrey Daniels, leading authority on performance management, calls this reaction to negative reinforcement "just enough to get by" behavior. In addition, he says you can immediately tell if you are in a negative reinforcement environment if you hear any of the following statements:

"That's what they get paid for."
"They oughta want to."
"It's **their** job. It's their responsibility."
"It's their fault."
"That's not my job."
"I've got too much."

One of the first actions you must take if you are trying to create a culture of high performance, innovation and creativity that can meet and exceed the demands placed upon you by your competition, customers and marketplace is to eliminate this negative talk from your organization. Train your leadership and employees in appropriate employee recognition. If the training fails, eliminate those with the attitudes.

Some common examples of negative reinforcement in the workplace are:

1) Negative feedback from your boss.

"You need to be producing ten more invoices a week or I am going to have to replace you." Performance increases to avoid the unpleasant circumstance of being replaced, but just to the required level.

2) Forced ranking/RIFs (reduction in force)

"We will be reducing our headcount by 10% at the end of the year." What usually results from a statement like this is performance improves until the RIF is over. Employees are trying to avoid the job loss, so productivity increases temporarily until the threat is gone. Unfortunately, other negative behaviors increase along with the productivity including sabotage, dishonesty and cheating.

Unlike positive and negative reinforcement which increase behaviors, punishers decrease or suppress a behavior. There are two methods of punishment. Using the first method, you decrease a behavior by administering an aversive stimulus. Some examples of this might include:

1) Management taking credit for what their employees have accomplished.

MBOs (management by objective) are a blatant example of this. Many corporations still have MBOs, the purpose of which is to recognize management fulfillment of their specific tasks and activities related to the corporate strategic goals. Once a year, the managers get big cash bonuses, they go and purchase new clothes, new cars and exotic vacations. Their subordinates watch as the second Christmas of the year happens for the elite class of the organization. If management is getting the reward, why should I do anything to improve? Why work hard when someone else is receiving the credit? This reinforcement strategy results in 70-80% of the workforce that does not care about the strategic goals, that does not focus on improving the process, and that probably does not even know or care what the corporate strategic goals are.

2)   Increasing the work load.

The boss needs a report in one day that which would normally take three days to compile. Ken "pulls out the stops" to get it completed on time; he skips lunch and takes work home. He completes the assignment on time. When presenting the report to his superior, Ken's boss brags that Ken was able to complete reports of this nature in one day. Result: Ken's in-basket fills up with similar requests. What Ken did as a special favor has turned into a nightmare.

3)   Discrediting an idea.

A manager brings his manufacturing group together to discuss their poor quality. Katy suggests that they put TQC (total quality control) checkpoints throughout their process, so they can check each other's work. The manager laughs at Katy and says, "Yeah, right. I can't get you to follow the work instructions, let alone follow a checksheet.". He asks for other ideas and wonders why none are forthcoming.

The second punishment method is to remove a positive reinforcer to decrease a behavior. Some examples of this method might include:

1) Take away hour lunches to decrease tardiness.
2) No more training until we decrease expenses.

As you can see by both these examples, something perceived as positive – one hour lunches and training opportunities – have been removed to decrease specific behaviors – tardiness and spending. Punishment simply suppresses a behavior temporarily, as long as the consequences or threat is in place. As parents, we should know this intuitively. Have you ever told your children "You cannot go anywhere (the positive reinforcer is the privilege of going out) until your bedroom is clean (decrease sloppiness)." What happens? They usually quickly clean their room, so they can go pursue their fun. Does the punishment make them keep their room clean forever? No. Does this punishment cause them to come up with ideas and plans for organizing their room or for having the cleanest room in the United States? No. The room is cleaned to the minimum possible standard required to get the positive reinforcement back (leaving the house).

Extinction is very simply ignoring a behavior causing it to stop. Effectively used, it can drive a decrease in unwanted behaviors such as employee complaining. If you are spending the majority of your time listening to one or two complaining employees, then your attention (positive reinforcement) is increasing this behavior. By removing your attention, the behavior will decrease. On the other hand, using extinction ineffectively, shuts down the discretionary efforts of your employees. If someone is doing outstanding work or is providing tons of new ideas and receives no attention or positive reinforcement, these behaviors will eventually disappear. No one likes to be taken for granted. Aubrey Daniels states *"Management changes behavior by its action and its inaction"*.

Although effective in some situations, not one of these rein-forcement methods – negative reinforcement, punishment or extinc-

The flip side - negative reinforcement and negative consequences

tion – will drive a person to their highest performance level. Consider the following facts:

- ✓ The American Psycholinguistic Society reports "A person's mind takes 48% longer to understand a negative statement than a positive one . . . thus, compliments become a dynamic force in motivating others.".

- ✓ It takes four instances of positive reinforcement to cancel out one punishment (study on teacher effectiveness by Madsen).

- ✓ In an informal survey conducted by Aubrey Daniels, he reports "Managers spend 85% of their time either telling people what to do, figuring out what to tell them to do or deciding what to do because employees did not do what they told them to do."

- ✓ Most negative reinforcers, punishers and uses of extinction occur unintentionally.

- ✓ Doing nothing is doing something.

- ✓ People repeat negative stories twice as often as they do positive ones.

- ✓ The person's resulting behavior after they receive a reinforcer determines whether it was a positive or negative consequence.

Regardless of whether the reinforcement methods you use are planned or accidental, you will "reap what you sow". The solution lies in training your people, requiring through their goals that management spends the majority of their time positively reinforcing what is good for the business, and having a recognition system that is immediately accessible and easy to use.

What do the experts say?

"We can communicate an idea around the world in 70 seconds, but it sometimes takes years for an idea to get through a quarter inch of human skull."

Charles Kettering, scientist and engineer

THERE are many experts on reinforcement whose research validates the need for effective recognition systems in the workplace.

Abraham Maslow

Maslow's studies teach us that we must take care of people's basic needs first – survival, safety, security and social interaction. After these needs are satisfied, we can work on helping people learn, grow and reach their fullest potential. Reaching the highest level requires motivation.

Frederick Herzberg

Herzberg's research shows that often we confuse "movement" with "motivation". An example he gives shows how negative reinforcement can be confused as motivation. *"Why is KITA (kick in the ass) not motivation? If I kick my dog from the front or the back, he will move. And, when I want him to move again, what must I do? I must kick him again. I can charge a man's battery, and then recharge it and recharge it again, but it is only when he has his own generator that we can talk about motivation."*

Douglas MacGregor

McGregor, an MIT professor, teaches us that managers need to operate under the following assumptions:

1) People are motivated to pursue what they perceive they need. So, to motivate our workforces, leaders must create and continually modify the work environment, so employees can fulfill their needs while pursuing what the business requires.

2) Managers must abandon their oversimplified, mechanistic view of the workplace (i.e. time clocks) and learn to deal with the human side.

3) Employees cannot be thought of as machine parts to be fixed, redesigned or eliminated when there are problems. Employees must be treated as individuals in all their complexities.

Aronson, Kunda, Baumeister, Greenberg, Pyszczynski – Experts on Self-Esteem

People have an underlying need to maintain a favorable image of themselves.

B.F. Skinner

There are two very important lessons we gain from Skinner's work. First, all of human behavior can be understood by examining the rewards and punishment in the environment. The second point, it may take as many as 50,000 reinforcers to teach a child basic math skills; this translates into 70 reinforcers an hour per student for the first four grades of school. This causes me to wonder how, by any stretch of the imagination, we can think once a year recognition or rewards can possibly work to change our cultures.

Aubrey Daniels

Daniels has two excellent books on performance management, **Bringing Out the Best in People, Performance Management** and **Improving Quality Productivity Through Positive Reinforcement.** These books make several important points including:

- ✓ Consequences determine behavior.
- ✓ You can't simply tell someone what to do over and over and over again.
- ✓ You cannot manage by common sense; each person's common sense is different as it comes from personal experience.
- ✓ Promises of rewards in the future do not work, such as annual raises, profit sharing, etc.; immediacy is a key to effective positive reinforcement.
- ✓ Goals must be broken down into specific "pinpointed" behaviors; positively reinforce progress.
- ✓ Management by best seller, what Daniels calls "fad fixes", will not work if you have not defined positive reinforcement, as well as eliminated negative consequences of the change.
- ✓ Regardless of what you are trying to accomplish in the workplace, employees and their behavior is involved.

These experts have made the study of behavior their life's work, so their findings and knowledge are important resources in creating an environment where people can learn, be creative and flourish. People and their behavior directly influence every business decision and result. Their behavior is always the result of reinforcement – the consequences. It is critical to understand how we can provide the consequences that drive the behaviors which will keep our businesses successful.

79

Section 2:
MYTHS

*Our scientific power has outrun our spiritual power.
We have guided missiles and misguided men.*

Rev Dr Martin Luther King Jr.

Myth #1:

Cash is the best recognition method

"The glow of one warm thought is to me worth more than money."

Thomas Jefferson

GRANTED, we are a materialistic society, but we must wake up to the realization that there are some things we just cannot buy. Discretionary effort is one of these things. The almighty buck will not buy the personal qualities or the environment needed for quantum change and our future success as a business. There is a plethora of information and research substantiating the case against cash. Some of the most compelling reasons include:

1) **You can never pay people enough or what they feel their contribution is worth.**

Have you ever heard anyone say, "Don't pay me that. It's too much!" History has shown us that if the money is given, we'll take it. For example, when General Motors was in its death spiral, the executives continued their bonuses which were extremely exorbitant considering the state of their business. When we receive our merit increases, do we ever say "I'm getting by just fine. Don't give me 7%. Let's go 5%; 5% will be just great!"? NEVER.

And, what about our ideas that yield the company financial benefits? I have an idea that saves my company $30K the first year it is implemented and the same amount for the following four years - a total of $150,000. How much money do you award me for this contribution? Should I receive 5% of the $30K or the $150K? Or, should I receive 5% of whatever is actually realized on an annual basis? Who pays the taxes on the award amount? What if other costs go up after a while due to the change? Is the contribution still as valuable? What if I have a safety idea that will prevent a work injury that has the potential of costing the company $1 million over the next 10 years? What do you pay me for cost avoidance? What if the forecasts or calculations are wrong? What if? How much? At what dollar amount will the employee feel valued and motivated? What dollar amount will make the employee feel cheated? What a nightmare!

2) **Research has proven that the impact of cash recognition is three to ten days; there is no "trophy" value.**

In contrast, the right non-cash recognition award can last a lifetime. How many professionals do you know that have their framed diplomas on their office walls? I also have kept special thank you cards, pictures, articles from newspapers that include my name, a "pretty rock" my oldest son gave me 20 years ago for "being a good mom," etc. What special things have you saved to remember your accomplishments? Ten years ago, I received $100 cash for an outstanding contribution. I am really not sure exactly what I spent the money on, probably a bill. I am not even exactly sure what I accomplished, as I have no keepsake. Money is "easy come, easy go." All of the profit sharing plans, annual bonuses and cash for ideas schemes in the world are not going to unlock the discretionary effort of your employees. These tools are too infrequent and the impact is fleeting. They are nice (an employee benefit) and useful in attracting new hires to our companies, but they are not effective positive reinforcement.

Myth #1: Cash is the best recognition method

3)   You can't get money quick enough.

In order to be effective, recognition must be immediate. Behavioral scientists have stated that the impact of the recognition decreases exponentially, the further away from the accomplishment it occurs. Although estimates of "no impact" range from one to two weeks, if you look at your systems for getting cash recognition, I am sure they are far from immediate. Bureaucracy ruins any chance of making a cash system work; there is paperwork, approval signatures, taxes, payroll has to cut the check, etc. Due to the red tape, many cash systems for awarding employees are set up on annual cycles, so if my improvement happens January 15, I will probably not be awarded until January of the next year, not even close to the effective range. Our corporate systems and the laws governing taxation and cash bonuses will never allow us to operate in the "immediate zone" required.

4)   Whenever money is offered for a result, the focus shifts from "doing the best job ever" to "getting the money as quick as possible".

People go to work because they need money. Once, a manufacturing operation fell drastically behind on their schedule due to a materials problem. Their solution was to offer each assembly associate $500 if they could get back on schedule in six weeks, before the end of the quarter. The assembly associates worked 10 hours a day, as well as every Saturday and Sunday (big overtime $$$). The first week, the number climbed. The second week, numbers were a little higher than usual. By the third week, production was just barely enough to meet the goal and mistakes began to surface. Tempers were flaring; the pressure was on. Well, the good news is they all received their money. The bad news is they were not motivated to a new, improved performance level. No new ideas surfaced. No process improvements occurred. No problems were solved. They simply worked longer and harder. And, a new precedent was set; the next time they fall behind they will expect a bonus.

Myth #1: Cash is the best recognition method

5)   Money is not a motivator.

In *One Size Fits One*, the authors share the following:

> "How do you go about creating this spirit? Money – frequently the first thing that comes to mind when thinking about ways to motivate people – is a factor but, as far as we're concerned, it's not the factor. Not even close.
>
> By way of illustration, we recently visited a number of outlets of a national restaurant chain where the pay was the same from restaurant to restaurant. Nevertheless, in some of the restaurants, the service was impeccable and the spirit bracing while, in others, the service was slap-dash and the only spirit to be had was in the drinks at the bar.
>
> What made the difference? Clearly not money in this case, since money was a constant. Rather, based on our own experience on the job, we have to assume that spirit originated where it almost always does – with leadership – the way each manager set expectations for employees, treated them as a team and as individuals and gave them the authority and the training necessary to get the job done. That, and encouraging everyone on the staff to choose to serve rather than serve to get. . . . Money was not a motivator - not a motivator, that is, to increased desire or greater caring."

The impact of money is fleeting; it definitely is not a keepsake. When you think about it, the assertion that "money is the root of all evil" is very true. It does not bring out our finest personal values and attributes. Our experience with cash recognition is that it brings the worst out in every person involved – the amount is not enough, the person who got the cash wasn't as deserving as I am – I work harder, etc. To bring your organization to its highest level, you must concentrate on the "heart", not the bank book.

Myth #2:
A salary is enough

*"It is NOT cash that fuels the journey to the future,
but the emotional and intellectual energy of every employee."*

*"It is senior management's responsibility to imbue work with a higher
purpose than a paycheck."*

Gary Hamel and C.K. Prahalad
Competing for the Future

*"Money is not the most important consideration for people at work. The
way people are treated at work is much more important for determining
performance than the money they receive."*

Aubrey Daniels
Bringing Out the Best in People

WE have already provided data on the very short-term impact of cash
(three-ten days).   If you are compensated biweekly or even weekly,
that is not enough motivation to sustain you between pay periods.
And, for the millions who live from paycheck to paycheck, stroking
out checks to pay the bills two days prior to payday, it is not motivating at all.   Aubrey Daniels captures the attitude well by saying,
"Whether you work hard today or whether you don't will make no

Myth #2: A salary is enough

difference in your paycheck." Our salaries are very simply financial consideration in exchange for completing a specific task or service.

We also know that when we hear "that's what they get paid for", we are in a environment of negative reinforcement and will never realize the benefit of maximized performance. This attitude squelches employee creativity and spirit, and should be eliminated if your goal is to tap into discretionary effort and employee potential.

There are several excellent examples which contradict this theory given in a book by Bill Catlette and Richard Hadden entitled **Contented Cows Give Better Milk.** Some of these facts include:

1) Look how our foreign competition has overtaken our marketplace in the last 30 years. Yet, American workers are the highest paid in the world.

2) Look at the New York Yankees in the 80s and early 90s. George Steinbrenner had the league high payroll and could not produce a championship team. In fact, many of these ball players were begging to be traded.

3) In 1983, the *St. Petersburg Times* (Florida) published a study of the correlation between pay and performance in the NFL and reported -

   ✓ The highest paid team in the NFL finished in last place.
   ✓ The three highest paid teams finished last, next-to-last and in the #21 position.
   ✓ The upper salary quartile produced no division winners.
   ✓ The lowest paid team won its division.

4) The Harvard Studies conducted at Western Electric by Elton Mayo showed the relationship between motivation and productivity. He found that the extent to which we do or do not fully contribute is governed more by attitude than by necessity, fear or economic influence.

Myth #2: A salary is enough

Examples from other sources support this information:

- Frederick Herzberg in an article called "How Successful Businessmen Handle People" published in the *Harvard Business Review*, cited salary as the leading source of employee dissatisfaction; achievement and recognition were the greatest employee satisfiers.

- The American Productivity and Quality Center (APQC) conducted a benchmarking study on motivation at identified best companies in the US; 75% of these companies used non-cash, pat on the back types of systems.

- In an article produced by Sunrise® Consulting Group, the authors report that a mere 9% of employees see a correlation between organizational success and a reward for them. Also, 60% of managers surveyed believe their compensation would NOT increase if their performance improved and if their people are paid the same whether they produce 50 widgets or 20, they will with few exceptions only produce 20.

- Gerald Graham, professor of management at Wichita State University, found that money was not a top motivator. When 1500 employees from a variety of work settings were surveyed and asked to rank order 65 potential motivators, they ranked "personalized, instant recognition from managers" as number one and "letter of praise written by the manager" as number two.

Neglecting employee recognition because they are already paid to do the job is the biggest management mistake that can be made. It may very well be the difference between a manager and a leader. Although we all go to work because we need a paycheck, study after study has proven that unless pay is grossly inadequate, moving us to

89

the safety and security section of the Maslow hierarchy of needs, recognition will always be more successful at revealing discretionary effort. As an employee, I want to be more than a paycheck. I want to have pride in the work I do and have others notice the special way I handle my tasks. In her book *Beyond Generation X*, Claire Raines puts in very succinctly, *"A paycheck isn't enough anymore."* Amen.

Myth #3:

Employee competition brings out the best in people

"Use what talents you possess; the woods would be very silent if no birds sang except those that sang best."

Henry Van Dyke

ALL of us have been raised in a competitive environment with sports heroes, political races, marketplace pressures, Gallup polls, even the race to the moon. It is no wonder that this approach has moved into our workplace. No matter how you look at it, a competition always has a winner and at least one loser. Competition is defined as rivalry and if you look further at the definition of rivalry, you will see it described as "one of two or more striving to have something only one can possess" (*Webster's Ninth New Collegiate Dictionary*). If asked whether you would prefer having one or two people working toward your business objectives or your entire employee population, I am sure you would answer "the whole population". Yet, in most US companies less than 5% of the employee base is recognized on an annual basis. Every person has the innate need to feel noticed and appreciated, so every person who makes a contribution toward the successful operation of the business, no matter how small, should receive recognition. If you only recognize or positively reinforce the "salesman of the year" or the "team of the year", the majority of your workforce has been left unappreciated and unmotivated.

In *One Size Fits All*, the authors state *"We have seen high-level executives expend considerable time and energy to win a Caribbean cruise, often doing things that they know are not in the best interests of their customers or their company – a cruise that, incidentally they could easily afford on their salaries but that they have to compete for (and win) to save face or elevate their standing within their organization."* In another section of the book, they state *"The arena where the most intense competition in business is often waged is within the corporation itself, among its employees."*

There are several good business reasons to eliminate competition in the workplace

1)   It costs too much to judge and score.

One company's system to recognize included the first-line manager preparing a one to two page justification letter which was sent to the director (third level of management) of the organization; this exercise took approximately two hours. Then, the director read all the nominations and screened them for finalists; this action took two to four hours depending on the number of nominations. If your employee was selected, you had to give a presentation at the director's staff meeting on why the employee was deserving; another two hours is spent preparing and delivering the presentation. Then, the staff listens to all the presentations, reviews each nomination and decides who should receive an award; this is a dozen second level managers and the director spending approximately four hours selecting recipients. And, the award process is still not over. There are two possible awards – a $50 award and a $100 award – so this high level staff decides who deserves which award; another hour is spent. Now, think of all the hours spent and the wages of the managers involved. Do you think it may have been more cost effective to just give all the nominees the $100? It would have been, by a long shot.

Myth #3: Employee competition brings out the best in people

2)   People focus on the "winning the big award" versus developing the best solution.

Competitions usually involve deadlines and a "race to the finish line", so you do not encourage taking the time required to arrive at the best solution, but getting a solution before anyone else can. Winning is the only thing that is important and people will take the quickest route to the award, lowering performance.

3)   Relationship problems develop.

- ✓   People guard their ideas and projects like Pentagon secrets which results in duplication of effort.
- ✓   The management theory that the winners will feel appreciated and the losers will try harder next time is totally false. The losers generally will not compete again. Winning is at the expense of our peers.
- ✓   Internal walls are built, slowing normal business operations and sometimes impacting the customer.
- ✓   Trust level is destroyed; when people lose they tend to justify the loss by thinking someone cheated, management was playing favorites, etc.
- ✓   Competitions often breed sabotage, back-biting, lying and cheating behaviors from people that are normally very honest and caring.

4)   Politics rule.

The management with the biggest empire usually influences the outcome of the competition and the distinction between the actual contributions of the winners and losers is minuscule. So, why discourage anyone? The more ideas and contributions we have, the better. Establishing a winner doesn't buy us anything. We learn and can gain from every contribution, so why would we discourage people? The difference between a winner and a loser may be $1 depending on your criteria.

3M, several times noted as a "best practice" company, does not believe in giving awards just for the ideas chosen for development, because doing so punishes the people whose ideas are not chosen. Your next greatest product idea could walk out the door tomorrow thinking, "They'll never go for this. The last time I had an idea, it was a loser."

5)   You demotivate more people than you motivate.

One company gave a presentation at a national conference about their team recognition package which awarded 17 teams annually. When asked what the employee population was, the audience was told "54,000". Then, they were asked how many teams the company had at present. The enthusiastic response was "hundreds." Not very good odds of being appreciated. And, with a company of 54,000, how do you compare the wide variety of contributions made by the hundreds of teams? You would have to compare intangible to tangible contributions, new product breakthroughs to improvements of existing products, sales contributions to manufacturing contributions to engineering contributions, apples to oranges. People should not have to compete for appreciation. And, with competitions, there is always a greater chance of losing than winning. Competitions destroy the pride and confidence we need all our employees to have in order to achieve their potential. This type of workplace mentality comes from our culture which is described by Dr. Betty Sue Flowers at the University of Texas - "In this culture, we always need an enemy to define who we are." This is a sad statement of our state of affairs, but seems to be true.

6)   The same people will win all the time.

Many companies have the "employee of the month" or the "salesperson of the year" type of competition. These plans do not work for many reasons. First, your top employee is probably always going to be your top employee. So, are you going to announce and publicize the same person winning the award time after time? No. You give it to second best the next time and third best the following time. After a while, the award loses its credibility. Second, particularly in sales awards, some individuals have distinct advantages, such as best territory, largest number existing accounts, best product, etc. The other salespeople know this and don't even try to compete. Third, we have to confess, some employees have jobs that are just more important to the overall success of the business. For example, a development engineer is probably the most important position at a high tech company. But, the fact is, without the sales and marketing staff, secretaries, assemblers, sourcing people, delivery functions, etc., the design contribution would never make a dollar. You cannot run a company with 2% of your employee base.

Most American companies have all the competition they could possibly need in the marketplace. Don't demoralize and demotivate your employees by subjecting them to rivalries and judgment in the workplace. You should be able to say, "This year 100% of our workforce received recognition! Every single individual made a valuable contribution to our company's success." Keep the competition external to your company. Internally, build bridges not walls. Your goal should be to have 100% of your workforce striving to make the business better, to make everyone successful, and to have a company of winners not a handful.

Myth #4:
Only star performers
deserve recognition

"The majority of us lead quiet, unheralded lives as we pass through this world. There will most likely be no ticker-tape parades for us, no monuments created in our honor. But that does not lessen our possible impact, for there are scores of people waiting for someone just like us to come along; people who will appreciate our compassion, our encouragement, who will need our unique talents. Someone who will live a happier life merely because we took the time to share what we had to give.

Too often we underestimate the power of a touch, a smile, a kind word, a listening ear, an honest compliment, or the smallest act of caring, all of which have the potential to turn a life around. It's overwhelming to consider the continuous opportunities there are to make our love felt."

Leo Buscaglia - Born for Love

IT is a very common belief that we should not recognize people for just "doing their jobs." Many managers believe that only star performers and those who go "above and beyond" should receive notice. There have been two recent scientific studies in the workplace, previously mentioned, which provided results showing only 10-20% of the workforce is working to their potential. Less than 2% are suffering "burn out". The remaining workers are doing "just enough to get by". If we only recognize the "stars," less than 5% of the corporate population will receive positive reinforcement – and guess what? – feeling appreciated and receiving positive reinforcement is an innate human need. We ALL need it.

I am sure that most of you have heard of the Hawthorne effect – some scientists changed the type of lights in an assembly environment and productivity went up. After a while, it returned to normal. Why did the productivity increase? Did the light bulbs do it? NO. It was the ATTENTION!!! All of us need attention and if it is not forthcoming, stars become mediocre performers (extinction) and no performance improvements will ever occur.

Part of the problem with this approach is how one defines "star" and "above and beyond" performance. Each individual is different (that's why we are called "individuals"). My outstanding performance level will never be the same as your outstanding performance level. And, my idea of what your job tasks are will probably never be identical to what your description is. My definition of a star will never be your definition of a star. My expectations are as unique as I am. Ask several individuals to give you the three attributes of a star performer and I am sure you will get different responses. Ask several managers what their expectations are of a star performer and I am sure these will vary as well. If you continue and ask, "Who is your star performer?" - most managers will provide you with the name of their top person easily. This is the problem. Our expectation is that there is only one star and our expectations can dramatically impact performance.

Robert Rosenthal, a psychologist and researcher from Harvard University conducted a study regarding the power of expectations on performance in South San Francisco elementary schools (study is published in *Pygmalion in the Classroom*). Rosenthal randomly selected 20% of the student body and told the teachers that these children had unusual potential for intellectual growth. Predictably, the teachers had higher expectations for these students and treated them differently than they did the other students. The students responded by learning at an accelerated pace and showed significantly more progress than their peers. Expectations can dramatically affect performance. So, if you are a manager and you expect to have one star performer, how many do you think you will have? One. It is a self-fulfilling prophecy and, although it may be subtle or unintentional, you can bet that you are throwing all kinds of positive reinforcement at that individual.

As parents, do you identify one child as the star? Let's say you are a parent with two children – one child gets straight A's in school, but has the messiest bedroom west of the Mississippi and refuses to take on the responsibilities required of a family member; your other child gets C's in school, but has the cleanest room and even helps with household chores without being asked. These are both good kids, but which one is the star? Which one gets the positive reinforcement? The correct answer is they both should. You try to reinforce what they are already doing well, so that it continues and you try to reinforce improvements in the behaviors you want to change.

Everyone possesses a "star" quality, but when you are recognizing just stars in your organizations, you have limited recognition to the expectations of the individual establishing the criteria. Recognition must not only let our stars know we appreciate their outstanding contributions; our systems must be designed to improve all individual performance to new high levels.

Star performers are generally rewarded with compensation increases and promotions based on specific results and deliverables. All of us have room for some type of improvement, which is the purpose for recognition and positive reinforcement. Recognition is NOT a benefit; it is the positive reinforcement that we use to drive the learning and change we need in our workplace and to celebrate achievement of our goals and objectives. We need every last one of our people striving toward business goals and objectives, if we are to survive in the future marketplace. Each one of us has some type of untapped potential waiting to be revealed.

What isn't recognition

"You cannot be a success in any business without believing that
it is the greatest business in the world. . .
If we believe that we are working for just another company,
then we're going to be like another company."

Thomas J. Watson, Sr.

WHEN designing an effective recognition system, it is important not only to define what recognition is, but to analyze existing tools to identify what you are currently using that is NOT recognition. Recognition is NOT:

● **A lottery.**

Recognition should never be a game of chance or luck. One corporation provided each manager with a pair of tickets to a major sporting event to award as recognition to a deserving employee. Instead of spending some time, deciding who should receive the tickets and planning to present them in a thoughtful manner, everyone's name was placed in a hat for a drawing. No specific behavior or practice was reinforced; the potential benefit was forfeited. In addition, the classic win/lose situation was created.

101

- **A quick, easy, low priority task.**

Recognition must be sincere, well-planned and properly executed. Do not take short cuts with one of the most valuable management tools in your possession! It takes time not only to identify those behaviors, practices and achievements critical to the success of your business, but to plan the appropriate recognition for each and how to deliver it in a meaningful, timely manner.

- **Boring.**

Celebrate successes in a way meaningful and exciting to the recipients. Nothing is worse than being invited to a stuffy awards ceremony or all-managers meeting. Having accomplishing a quality improvement, achieving a goal or completing a project, there is need for closure, the need to brag about and share what you have accomplished, the need to let your hair down and the need to gain the momentum required to undertake a new endeavor. Tom Peters has said, *"Celebrate what you want to see more of "*.

- **A regularly, scheduled activity.**

"We will recognize one employee per quarter at the all managers meeting." This is definitely the wrong approach. Recognition should be as spontaneous and timely as possible. New habits do not develop overnight, so until you integrate recognition into your daily activities, you may want to actually schedule time on you calendar at the end of your day to say "thank you". Always remember, the longer you wait to recognize the behavior, principle or practice, the less impact your reinforcement will have.

- **A replacement for compensation (and vice versa).**

Both the recognition system and the compensation system

What isn't recognition

need to be applied consistently and equitably. One without the other does not work. Remember, however that reward and recognition are not synonymous; they address two entirely different needs. Providing a good salary to an employee will never replace their need to feel appreciated.

- **A raise in wages.**

Salary raises are not frequent or timely. They are usually scheduled events and may follow months after an achievement. A cash exchange for a service is not appreciation, it is financial consideration in exchange for performance of designated tasks. It lacks the sincerity and warmth associated with a "thanks".

- **Giving stock options or gain sharing.**

These are parts of a compensation package. They are not presented immediately, warmly or sincerely. They are not flexible. Often, stock options and bonuses are given on the basis of length of service or position in the corporate food chain, neither of which reinforces any specific individual behaviors or practices other than "being there" and "being where".

- **Improving the benefits package.**

This is another compensation package feature given to everyone. It does not reinforce a specific practice or principle.

- **Something given to everyone - the turkey, holiday bonus, form letter . . .**

These once a year or term vehicles are not frequent or sincere. You may save time in planning and execution, but you sacrifice the great benefits and gains associated with reinforcing a specific behavior or practice.

103

- **Anything forced or automatic; anything perceived as insincere.**

Regularly scheduled vehicles, such as service awards, which are not presented in a celebration environment lose their impact. Often, in large companies, these awards are distributed through the mail. Recognition should be accompanied with great fanfare. Any tool perceived as automatic sacrifices its intent.

Take a moment to think about your current workplace practices that are called "recognition". If they do not meet the criteria for recognition including all three A's (acknowledgment, approval and appreciation) and all seven characteristics for effective recognition (sincere, fair/consistent, timely, frequent, flexible, appropriate, specific), you will need to redesign your system or modify your tools. You will probably see many opportunities for immediate improvement. It begins with your philosophy, principles and what you want to achieve.

If you want to drive a culture change or implement a new method of conducting your business, make sure that you are not recognizing the wrong things, at the wrong time, with the wrong tool. If you want widespread change and to tap into 100% of your potential talent, make sure your tools are set up to recognize the majority. And, don't ever make employee recognition the first thing you cut, along with training, when times get rough and you need cost savings. Lean times require more positive reinforcement.

Section 3:
METHODS

Take away my factories, and I will build a new and better factory; but take away my people and grass will grow on the factory floor.

Andrew Carnegie

Developing your unique recognition strategy

Listen.
In every office
you hear the threads
of love and joy and fear and guilt,
the cries for celebration and reassurance,
and somehow you know that connecting those threads
is what you are supposed to do
and business takes care of itself.

from the poem entitled Threads
by James A. Autrey

THE process for developing a recognition system unique to your specific business requirements is very simple. The five step process is

1) Determine what you want to achieve.

2) Identify what you will recognize.

3) Select your recognition tools.

4) Show you care.

5) Measure, monitor and continuously improve your recognition processes.

Step one:
Determine what you
want to achieve

"If you want someone to do a good job, give them a good job to do."

Frederick Herzberg
Alignment of Goals

MOST companies will already have part of this step completed. Most of us have defined our vision, mission, strategy, goals and objectives. It is important that all of these items are "aligned" and that they are cascaded and translated into "meaningful" individual behaviors, actions and goals. Usually, around the first of the year, we stop to review our performance over the past 12 months and look into our "crystal ball" to see which direction we should go to be successful in the future. We establish new budgets, make resolutions for the new year, formulate strategic plans and begin the cascade of goals down through the entire organization. It is critical that goals are cascaded effectively, so that every functional group supports each other and we achieve what is termed "alignment".

'Alignment' is described in *Webster's Ninth New Collegiate Dictionary* as "the proper positioning of parts in relation to each other". Our companies have a large number of "parts" – businesses, products, services and processes. In order to become more **aligned**,

Step one: Determine what you want to achieve

the first action is to establish the corporate direction, identify the common denominators and divide the work into functional contributions. The next action is aligning the specific functional group by setting high level goals which compliment and support the corporate goals. For instance, if the company sets a goal for revenue on a particular product next year, marketing must identify and secure the market, development must have the product to general availability in a certain length of time, manufacturing must produce the products, and so forth. Alignment occurs when all parts of our team provide their specific ingredient to the functional group's recipe for success. Now, the goals are cascaded down through the management chain to the individual department level, where they are finally translated into individual performance goals and development plans. These goals must be "meaningful" – something the individual can personally impact with their daily work. This translation is the critical success factor. You want your recognition system to provide effective positive reinforcement for those behaviors and actions that support what is good for the business. You want to drive the changes and encourage the learning that will help you reach your goals efficiently.

Mark Graham Brown, author and examiner for the Malcolm Baldrige National Quality Award, reports that best in class companies limit their goals to three or four to ensure the appropriate focus is given to critical business objectives. Every business, from pizza delivery to the US Postal Service, should have a maximum of four basic goals to meet. These goals are driven from customer requirements – cost, timeliness and quality, and from employee requirements or the cultural elements of our operations. So, when establishing goals, the most simple method is to evaluate what you are currently doing and ask:

Cost
- ✓ What part of our current process costs the most?
- ✓ What activities do we have that do not add value to our output?
- ✓ How can we make our output more valuable?

Timeliness
✓ What part of our current process takes the longest?
✓ Where are we holding the greatest amount of inventory and how can we reduce this amount without impacting schedule?

Customer/Quality
✓ What is our major quality or customer issue?
✓ What do our competitors offer that we don't?
✓ What process improvement would be the most noticeable and pleasing to the customer?

Employee/Cultural
✓ What is the greatest obstacle/barrier to my being the most effective and satisfied?
✓ What would help me complete my job quicker, more consistently, at a reduced cost and/or with a higher personal satisfaction level (i.e. training, equipment, software, etc.)?

The keys to being successfully aligned are to

1) Remember that you are only one part of the recipe; without the other ingredients (functions), the job does not get done.
2) Keep it simple; keep goals to a minimum.
3) Stay focused on what is good for the business.
4) Establish meaningful goals; show every individual how they can have a positive, direct impact on the success of the business.

Alignment is not a new buzzword. It has been and will always be the key for running a successful business. Being aligned is simply having the right recipe (goals), the right ingredients (people and functions), the right tools (methods and machines), the right reinforcement and the right timing. It is achieved by the proper identification of where you fit in relationship to the other parts of the business and the development of meaningful goals reinforced with recognition for milestones that improve and support relationships and business requirements.

Goals: Fact and Fiction

After reviewing the myths surrounding recognition processes, it is not surprising to find that there are several myths about goals that we subscribe to in the workplace.

1)   **Goals are inspirational.**

Goals are antecedents; goals simply tell us what to do. Behavior, as discussed previously, is determined by consequences – particularly, the immediate reinforcement we receive. This should be intuitive to most of us. How many of you exceed the speed limit, smoke, eat too much, have unhealthy items in your diet, drink eight glasses of water a day, don't exercise, etc.? Yet we have been told over and over again that if we quit smoking, drive safely, drink water, eat right and exercise, we will live longer. And, these things are not a matter of making a 1% difference in our merit increases; these behaviors are a matter of life.

2)   **Goals should be established and evaluated annually.**

The first problem with annual goals is that they can be discouraging or seem unachievable. For example, John is working hard to make two widgets a day. His boss brings him into the office and says, "Your goal for next year is to make ten widgets a day." John thinks, "Ten widgets! I am killing myself to get two – I'll never make that goal." So, he writes it off as an impossibility. What if John's boss said, "I'd like you to be able to reach three widgets a day. Let's identify what obstacles keep us from doing that and work on them". Maybe,

John achieves the goal in a week or maybe, he achieves it in a month. The important point is that the goal is believable; John can see increasing to three widgets. This is the approach used by the very successful Weight Watchers™ program. It is easy to get discouraged and give up when your goal is to lose 100 pounds; make smaller, short-term goals and recognize progress.

The second problem with annual goals is that they enable the individual to procrastinate. Why should John produce ten widgets a day for the next 11 months (more work), when he doesn't have to produce to that level until just prior to his next evaluation? The solution is to set goals in smaller increments, recognize each milestone and eliminate time expectations. You may be surprised at what you can achieve with this method.

3) **The same goal for everyone will enable the department to reach its goals.**

This is the "lazy boss" approach. Every person is unique; we all have different areas that require improvement. Consider John again; he currently produces two widgets a day. Joe, his co-worker produces nine a day. So, the boss gives all his/her employees a "ten widgets a day" goal. For Joe, this is barely a challenge, but for John it seems impossible. John resents this pressure, because he never makes a mistake, so, in reality, his work is getting to the customer before Joe's. Even though his daily count is higher, Joe has approximately 50% of his work returned for repair. The organization's goal is reduce production cycle time by 10%. Repairs more than double the cycle time. So, the smart approach is to make John's goal to increase parts per day and Joe's goal should be to decrease his return rate. Both goals should be gradual and positive reinforcement given for progress. As each

Step one: Determine what you want to achieve

person improves their specific contribution, the overall department objective will be realized.

4)   More goals are better.

As mentioned before, each person should have four goals maximum. The more goals you have, the less you can focus. Identify what actions would be the most important to the success of your business right now ("biggest bang for the buck") and concentrate on these. The goals should be broken into short-term milestones or goals that you can continuously monitor and recognize. We can't be in ten places at once or work on ten improvements at one time. Focus is the key word.

If we examine the flip side of the myths about goals, we can determine the facts surrounding goal setting, including:

✓   Goals must be meaningful to the individual.

The goal should be something the individual can personally impact during his/her daily activities.

✓   Goals must cascade.

It is important to understand how achievement of your goals benefits the company. No matter how minimal the impact, enabling the employee to see that he/she has a positive influence on the big picture, reinforces the feeling of personal importance and value.

✓   Goal-setting is a continuous process.

Goals are achieved every day, so why do we conduct goal-setting exercises once a year? The very minute we achieve a goal, we should celebrate and move on, either by establishing a new goal in the same specific area (cost, timeliness, quality, employee/culture) or by having the individual concentrate on achieving another existing goal. The important thing is not waiting until it is too late to recognize the achievement.

✓ Goals must be measurable and visible.

You can measure almost any process in the workplace. Remember, even though it is very subtle, just seeing performance improve on a chart is a form of positive reinforcement. Have employees measure themselves to realize the greatest benefit from metrics. This helps them see immediately how they are performing, which enhances learning, trust and feedback skills. Having clear, concise and understandable goals can make or break the effectiveness of your recognition system.

✓ Aubrey Daniels suggests that when developing initiatives, strategies and goals, the manager should

1) Identify what individual behaviors are required for the change to be successful,
2) Identify how the current individual behavior(s) will be impacted by the change,
3) Ensure that you have eliminated or lessened the negative consequences, and
4) Provide for both immediate positive reinforcement and negative consequences for the associated behavior required.

In Beyond Generation X, by Claire Raines, an account is given on how the Air Force Academy has changed their goal-setting process. They have reduced individual goals to verbal contracts of 30 days. This contract between employee and manager includes: "what we'll give you" and "what we require in return". Although simple this process exemplifies the method we need to institute to make our goal-setting and recognition systems more effective.

Step two:

Identify what you will recognize

"Management needs to identify those systems and behaviors that employees perceive to be inequitable and destroy them. Then, they should formulate a theory that describes the type of environment in which people can learn, grow and make a contribution and persist in making it happen."

One Size Fits All
Gary Heil, Tom Parker & Deborah C. Stephens

Opportunities for Recognition

BEHAVIORS, activities and achievements that deserve to be recognized cover a wide spectrum, from displaying an attitude that has a positive impact to completing projects with outstanding measurable results. Remember, a state-of-the-art recognition system is flexible, accommodates a variety of different situations, and gives you the ability to say at the end of the year "We recognized 100% of our employees!" Realize that any job well done is worth recognizing, and any behavior we appreciate and would like to see repeated is worth taking the time to say "Thank you!" AIM Management Group in Houston, Texas defines their recognition opportunities as any work behavior or practice "worthy of admiration". Some opportunities might include recognizing those:

117

Step two: Identify what you will recognize

- ✓ Having a positive impact on co-workers
- ✓ Applying a process improvement tool effectively
- ✓ Showing initiative
- ✓ Displaying teamwork
- ✓ Demonstrating extra effort
- ✓ Volunteering
- ✓ Identifying the solution to a recurring problem
- ✓ Proposing an idea
- ✓ Improving the work environment
- ✓ Reaching milestones toward goal achievement.

Try to realize that, in general, we have very high expectations of ourselves and others. It is important to avoid missing opportunities to say "thanks!" If you are questioning "Should I or shouldn't I?" – the answer is probably "You should!"

Clearly define the purpose of your recognition system, review your business objectives, establish individual goals and then develop lists of behaviors, activities and milestones that support your mission. For instance, an example of a recognition system purpose might be

> *"To acknowledge and appreciate those behaviors and practices that establish a working environment that promotes the concepts of loyalty, belonging, confidence, self-worth, teamwork, respect, creativity and trust, as well as having a positive impact on business goals and objectives, through frequent and sincere methods of approval."*

As a manager, you know the long-term objectives for your department. You simply take each goal/objective and break it down into the behaviors, actions and milestones that you will recognize in order to expedite achievement. For example, if your goal is to reduce cycle time by 10% while maintaining the current quality level, you may identify the following lists:

118

Step two: Identify what you will recognize

BEHAVIORS	ACTIONS	MILESTONES
Makes suggestions. in staff meeting	Conducts a benchmarking project.	Cycle time reduction reaches 2%.
Reorganizes work area to eliminate roadblocks.	Simplifies and rewrites a procedure.	Cycle time reduction reaches 4%.
Volunteers for action items.	Completes training which will enhance efficiency.	Cycle time reduction reaches 6%.
Moves to critical path in process; helps others.	Creates a cross-training plan to increase flexibility.	Cycle time reduction reaches 8%.
Perfect attendance.	Develops a measurement system to prioritize all obstacles.	Cycle time reduction totals 10%.

This is simply a guideline. Some of the best things that happen are not anticipated and are unplanned, so do not limit yourself to a chart. The important thing is that you never miss an opportunity to recognize the behavior, actions and milestones that are moving you in the direction of your goal. Effectively recognizing these achievements will help you reach your goal in record time.

Who is Responsible for Recognition?

Although managers must serve as role models and should have effective use of positive reinforcement as one of their goals, make recognition the responsibility of everyone in the workplace. Design the processes so that anyone can initiate the recognition. Develop guidelines and training for all employees. If you limit the recognition responsibility to the management team, the results you get may be the results you have always had. It is unfair to the management, unfair to the people and unfair to the company which loses the benefits, which potentially include a highly focused and positive workforce. There are many relationships in the workplace that can be enhanced by giving everyone the ability to say "thank you" – our

119

relationships with customers, suppliers, peers, management, benchmarking partners, and those in our professional networks.

The main argument against an employee-driven system involves a lack of trust – "They will spend too much money!" or "They won't get their work done!" Be assured, with the proper amount of forethought and time spent in developing and piloting your system, you can build integrity into your processes. Most of the time, you will be surprised at how people can act responsibly when given the authority of being empowered and entrusted with obligations. In our experience, the benefits of this approach far outweigh any losses you may incur from abuse.

Managers, of course, are ultimately responsible for achievement of business results. Their focus needs to shift to creating an environment full of positive reinforcers that bring out the creativity and innovation of their reports versus telling people what to do and disciplining them when they do not meet expectations (i.e. military style managing). The environment required is one that sets people up for success. Management should receive extensive training in performance management, human behavior and positive reinforcement. Following this, they should be rated on how they positively reinforce (recognize) their employees and how the employees perceive their workplace and leader.

When Should I Say "Thank You"?

Though the reality is all of us have bad work habits that are embarrassing when held up for public review, we always find it more than a little amusing when someone asks "When do I say thank you?". It happens at nearly every presentation we have given. The answer is "When you feel like it!" We get so caught up in the day-to-day performance of our assigned tasks, that we do not notice the little things our co-workers do to make it easier to do our jobs and to create a better work environment. As mentioned previously, it is so much easier to identify the star performer and major achievements, and totally overlook the less obvious consistent contributions exemplifying teamwork, quality improvement, creativity, innovation, leadership and initiative that enable the success of our teams, departments and corporation on a daily basis. Every company is filled with "behind the scenes" individuals who are busy contributing to the success of the whole; without these individuals, we would fail miserably.

The easiest way to develop good recognition habits is to create a matrix, like the one shown previously, to help you identify positive steps toward your goals. Then, scribble notes in a day timer, calendar or notebook every time you witness a contribution indicating progress toward your objectives. Finally, schedule time at the end of each day and challenge yourself to identify an individual or team that has made your work day a little nicer, your tasks a little easier, your processes a little better, your environment a little more organized or brighter, or even made you a little smarter. The key is "a little more". Positively reinforcing progress helps us achieve goals quicker and yields a better return on our investment of time and resources. Many times, these individuals may not be "stars", but they definitely have a positive impact on your effectiveness, productivity and/or attitude. We are sure, if you are truly committed to changing and improving performance and work life, you will find more opportunities than you will ever be able to address. Decide what behaviors or practices you want to see occur more frequently and recognize them. If you are not achieving your objectives, you are reinforcing the wrong thing and need to reexamine the existing consequences. The results you achieve will always be the behaviors, practices and principles you are reinforcing.

Wrong Result = Reinforcing the Wrong Thing

Let's look at some real-life scenarios of behaviors we reinforce that do not give us what we really want, but give us what we are asking for:

What we really want is high quality work to go to our customer.

> In one department, an "employee of the month" award is given for successfully completing 20 working days without having an error. This honor comes with $100 cash and a designated parking place. Carol has made it

19 days and six hours. Suddenly, a customer brings back an error. It really isn't Carol's fault, it was caused by faulty equipment. It is considered an "error" as defined by the data collection procedure. Error measurements, however, are self-collected. To make matters even more difficult, Carol just discovered her daughter needs orthodontic work and she is going to have to come up with a $300 down payment. Several employees use this same piece of equipment and the problem causing the error will be identified eventually. Carol knows exactly what is wrong with the equipment as this same thing happened a year ago, but she needs the money and to get management to pay attention to the quality of her work. She hides the customer return and falsifies her measurements.

What we really get is a normally honest employee seduced by money into a dishonest behavior and several more errors going to the customer before the problem is resolved.

What we really want is to meet corporate strategic goals.

Many corporations still have management bonuses, the purpose of which is to recognize management fulfillment of their specific tasks and activities related to the corporate strategic goals. Once a year, managers receive the cash bonuses, go shopping and purchase new clothes and new cars, and take vacations. Their subordinates all watch as the second Christmas of the year occurs for the elite class of the organization. If management is getting the reward, why should I do anything to improve? Why work hard when someone else is receiving the credit?

What we really get is 70-90% of the workforce who do not care about the strategic goals, who do not focus on improving the processes related to achieving the goals, and who probably do

Step two: Identify what you will recognize

not even know or care what the corporate strategic goals are. We could be reaching the goals quicker and with more long-term solutions if we tapped the greatest resource – the people who actually perform the work, who make the difference.

What we really want is good teamwork and cooperation.

The majority of companies we have visited only have recognition tools in place for individual contributors, yet all of their training points to the obvious advantages of operating in a team. An employee has a great idea and could really use someone with a broader view of the business to ensure that any negative impact the idea might have on another functional process is addressed. The only recognition available is a "trip for two" award and those awards are only given to individuals. There is no comparable team award. Should the employee ask management to organize a team and get the experts needed to fine-tune the idea, or go ahead and implement without this input to get the trip?

What we really get are workers with ideas and methods that they guard like top secret Pentagon information. Many of these ideas are good, but lack the depth and experience that a team would bring to the final product. A "trip for two" is an extravagant gift, making it more like compensation than recognition and more like seduction and temptation to do the wrong thing than motivation to move the company forward in the best direction possible. The practice of recognizing only individuals promotes the "prima donna" approach to working. Equivalent individual and team recognition tools should be available to promote the multitude of efforts a business needs to be successful.

What we want are loyal employees.

Have you ever completed some monumental project and when someone at a high level in the corporate

123

Step two: Identify what you will recognize

structure gives positive feedback, your manager or someone else steps up to take full credit? It has been said that the great leader is not the one in the spotlight, he's the one leading the applause, yet managers have not been recognized or rewarded for the number of their employees with great ideas. They are promoted on the basis of personal merit and achievement. Naturally, they take as much credit as possible.

What we get are demotivated employees who hold management in low regard.

What we want is the strength, effectiveness and efficiency of a team.

One process improvement team solved a critical manufacturing problem, reducing the scrap rate and cycle time of a process. The manager took the whole team to lunch as a "thank you". Everything was going smoothly until the manager stood up at the end of the lunch and presented the team leader with a $100 gift certificate. As stated before, most company recognition programs and practices are designed for individual recognition, and even companies which have team recognition vehicles have erred by selecting an individual from a team to receive a higher level of recognition than the rest of the team members. This is taboo! As a general practice, all team members should be given the same level of recognition. Recognition for a "most valuable player" on a team should only be given on an exceptional basis and only when driven by a spontaneous expression of the team members.

What we really get is everybody fighting to be the team leader and people unwilling to make contributions to the team if they are not the leader.

124

What we want is the best person for the job, working to their full potential and capability.

> Kenneth has been assigned a big project which involves months of studying books and texts, and sorting all the information into a formal research paper. The project will take Kenneth eight to 12 months to accomplish; his manager gives him a deadline of a year. Kenneth really works hard, makes many personal sacrifices and spends every free minute at night and weekends working the project. At the eight month mark, the boss checks up on progress and Kenneth reports that he will probably be done in a week. The boss says, "That's why I gave you this project. It is so easy for you to do these reports.". Kenneth thinks, "Easy??? He thinks this was easy!". Kenneth's work has been underestimated, the value of his contribution minimized and his motivational level destroyed with one thoughtless and casual remark. Effective recognition can be as simple as asking, "How did you ever accomplish this?". This gives the person the ability to share what they have been doing and experiencing. Then, the manager can ensure the person receives the appropriate credit for their hard work.

What you really get is a disengaged employee who will never put forth his best effort again.

Our comments to each other in the workplace are critical. James Autrey, former *Fortune 500* executive, wrote many personal notes to his employees over the years. When one of his employees won $5,000 in the lottery, he wrote her a note of congratulations and added "I hope you won't take your earnings and leave us. We need you here.". Years later, at his retirement, she approached him with tears in her eyes. "I'll never forget that note you wrote me," she said. Our words are very powerful and sometimes they stay with others for a lifetime making it very important to watch what we say about the work and performance of others.

If you want these same behaviors and practices, keep with your old methods of operation. If you want to change the look of things, carefully consider what, who, where, when and how you plan to recognize and look for a different approach.

There are a great number of ways to recognize contributions in the workplace. When you think of personal experiences as a first-line manager, do you remember feeling like you were between a rock and a hard place? Do you recall thinking, "What a thankless job! I am getting it from both ends, my subordinates and my superiors. I can't win." And, what about being a supplier? Sometimes it feels like you could walk across water and your customer would then ask "But, are you impervious to fire?" Your peer relationships should be considered, too. Recognition tools and methods should be in place to make recognition possible in any direction – up and down the chain of command, across functions, internal and external to the company and among peers.

So often, your managers, fellow workers, suppliers and customers seem like traffic cops – the only time they pull you over is to tell you what you have done wrong. Is it any wonder we feel like we've been through the wringer by the time we get home at night? One good lesson to learn is to always look for the best in everyone, for everyone is special in some way. That is the key to finding opportunities to recognize. Instead of limiting our communication and efforts to finding what is wrong with everyone, we must refocus our attention on what is right with everyone. In addition, we must identify and positively reinforce what is "goodness" for the business. Is it being a team player and cooperating, or is it being a solo act? Is it having the elite few concentrating on corporate strategies or having the entire employee population focused on critical business objectives? Is it operating with trust, credibility and respect or operating outside of these principles? First, change your communication focus and the way you look at others. Then, identify what is good for the business and begin to develop your recognition plan. You will have no trouble finding the behaviors, actions and milestones to recognize – the opportunities are infinite.

Step three:
Select your recognition tools

"Managing people comes down to finding, motivating, growing, guiding, and keeping talent."

The Discipline of Market Leaders
Michael Treacy and Fred Wiersema

Considerations When Selecting a Recognition Vehicle

AS mentioned, recognition opportunities are too numerous to count. Your desired results will be achieved quicker and will be greater than ever before, if you have identified the right behaviors and actions to recognize, as well as the right tools for the right person and situation. Create a toolbox of recognition vehicles, so that you will have a method available for every situation. It wouldn't make sense to recognize a team who had realized a savings of $500,000 by improving their process with the same recognition vehicle you give an individual for reorganizing a file cabinet. And you definitely do not want to tie recognition with a dollar amount or return-on-investment, for there are several intangible efforts that are difficult to measure, but may be equally important to the organization. As stated repeatedly, effective recognition is not an easy or quick task. There are several considerations, but the two most important are:

127

Step three: Select your recognition tools

✓ **What is being recognized?**

The type of recognition selected should be proportionate to the activity. If the activity represents a significant accomplishment and the recognition is perceived as insignificant, its effect could be extremely demotivating. On the other hand, a tremendous acknowledgment for a small accomplishment not only seems insincere and inappropriate, it creates a false expectation of the same in the future. Always try to keep the focus on sincere appreciation versus the perceived dollar value of the award. Ensure that people understand that recognition is not a replacement for compensation. When someone achieves the outrageous or spectacular, they should receive a boost in their pay along with great fanfare and recognition.

✓ **What type of recognition would be valued by the recipient?**

The personal touch is the most important aspect of recognition. Knowing what the recipient values is a major part of the decision. Someone in an office environment may appreciate a certificate, wall plaque or desk accessory, while someone working in a clean room environment would have no place to display this type of recognition.

You can develop several types of recognition vehicles, suitable to either individual recognition or team recognition. Determining the appropriate vehicle is very important. The type of recognition selected must match the level of accomplishment or behavior achieved. As the significance of the contribution increases, so should the type of recognition.

Although management involvement in approval is sometimes required, systems should not be management-driven. *Anyone should be able to initiate any vehicle;* create an employee-driven recognition system. A matrix provides some guidelines, so that recognition tools are used consistently and responsibly. The important thing to note is that every possible type of contribution should be covered from

128

personal behaviors to major corporate contributions. If one category is inappropriate, another one is suitable. Instead of management saying "no" to a recognition opportunity, if the award suggested seems excessive, they have the ability to suggest an alternative. Everyone gets recognized. Although you may adjust your awards according to your budget, always limit the perceived value of recognition. Any extraordinary contribution meriting additional attention should be recognized with an award and rewarded with a compensation increase. If you exceed a certain perceived value, regardless of whether the award is cash or a gift (i.e. trips, cars, expensive jewelry, etc.), the recognition becomes reward – another form of compensation. The following sections will provide you with some ideas for recognition vehicles to satisfy all kinds of contributions.

Tried and True Approaches

<u>Required Features</u>

Ensure that all of your tools have the following features:

- ✓   There is a minimum of management approval required.

- ✓   The awards have limited perceived values; they are simply tokens of appreciation.

- ✓   The recognition is flexible enough that one may find an appropriate award for anyone and for any work-related behavior, value or personal impact that is deemed helpful or exemplary of good working practices or habits.

- ✓   Although we often consider these tools as management vehicles to enhance performance, all employees can use these methods to enhance relationships with customers, suppliers, superiors, subordinates, network associates or peers.

Step three: Select your recognition tools

It is important that there are tools available for all your identified recognition opportunities. All tools must meet the criteria established by the definition, purpose and seven characteristics of recognition, and be readily accessible and easy to use. Some examples of proven effective recognition techniques follow.

Tools for Day to Day Recognition

Thank You Cards

Thank you cards are an effective way to tell others how we appreciate something they have done for us. We use them in our personal lives and they can be used just as effectively as a person-to-person method of recognition in the workplace. The beauty of the "thank you" is that it is simple, spontaneous, immediate and can be used to recognize anyone.

Design an attractive thank you card using high quality stationery and colorful graphics, and include a company or organizational logo with a blank space inside for a handwritten message. Make it something that individuals will be proud to display in their offices. Add a matching envelope to make the thank you cards vehicles for external, as well as internal use. Thank you notes should be placed in locations convenient to all employees, where it takes no longer than a minute to retrieve it. We placed our thank you card racks by the coffee machine and at the entrance to the bathrooms, knowing every person would see them at least once a day and be reminded to appreciate their co-workers. Encourage the giver to take the thank you note and personally present it to the recipient, when possible, further reinforcing the behavior, value or practice. The following are a few examples of behaviors and attributes that might be recognized with this method:

Step three: Select your recognition tools

- Caring/respectful
- Displaying creativity/innovation
- Showing customer-focus
- Putting forth extra effort
- Flexibility
- Identifying a potential quality problem
- Providing special assistance or support
- Exhibiting initiative or leadership
- Actively participating
- Positive attitude
- Approachable
- Taking a risk
- Being a team player
- Making a time sacrifice
- Serving as an idea-generator
- Demonstrating resourcefulness.

Does this method seem a little too simple to be called recognition? Let's see if it fits our criteria.

✓ **The definition of recognition.**

Appreciation – it is a thank you note. Acknowledgment – the message states specifically why I am thanking the individual; my name and the recipient's name have been personally handwritten, as well as the behavior or practice. Approval – I liked what the recipient did so well that I took time to personally write the message and in some cases, deliver it.

✓ **The purpose of recognition.**

If I have thanked a peer for helping me proof a document, I have reinforced the concept that teamwork makes a better product, and the individual's worth to me by noting their skills, talents and willingness to help that I appreciate. These attributes are included in the purpose of recognition.

131

Step three: Select your recognition tools

✓ **The seven characteristics of recognition.**

1) Sincere – the message is from the heart, not the pocket book or the copying machine.

2) Fair and consistent – everyone is included and any work-related behavior or practice that a person values can be recognized with a thank you card.

3) Timely – it is immediate.

4) Frequent – you can write or receive as many thank you notes as warranted.

5) Flexible – it can fit any internal or external situation.

6) Appropriate – there is never a situation when a thank you or sincere appreciation is inappropriate. In fact, no matter what is being appreciated or what token of appreciation you are using, it should be required.

7) Specific – the behavior or practice that is valued is handwritten in the card.

As you can see, the thank you card process addresses all the criteria, requires little training and can be implemented easily. This is a good starting point for your new philosophy and policy on recognition. Whenever you create a new recognition tool or method, analyze its effectiveness by breaking it down into the critical components shown above and ensure that what you are planning is effective recognition.

One of the vice presidents in a corporation where a thank you card system was implemented stated during the presentation for management approval, "This is too corny! I guess we can try it if the team is convinced it will help." One month after implementation, he received his first thank you card and came running out of his office to show it to everyone close by. Anyone witnessing the event would have thought he had just won the state lottery. He carefully mounted the card on his wall to display. Today, several other thank you cards have joined that first message and he can proudly boast that he is the VP with the most. They remain on his wall as a constant reminder to him of what is important – a sort of living memorial to his management style and being people-oriented. Management used to be a thankless job or maybe people did appreciate certain leadership behaviors, but did not have the vehicle to express themselves.

Tokens

Tokens are funny money. There are several novelty manufacturers which will produce your coins or currency. The token can be any nominal amount – $1, $5, or even one hour time off. Tokens should never be redeemable for cash. Token systems can be designed so that recipients can collect several for higher redemption awards. For example, one token may be redeemed for a coffee mug, a lunch or a logo pen. Ten tokens can be exchanged for tickets to a ball game, an extra day vacation or dinner for two at a fine restaurant. If your corporation is large, you can bring attention to other internal businesses by allowing tokens to be redeemed there. For example, the tokens can be redeemable for special classes, wellness center, day care center, cafeteria, company store, etc.

Due to the fact that tokens have a perceived value, certain measures and monitoring must take place including:

1. Require that only one token may be given per thank you card.

2. Tokens must ALWAYS be accompanied by a personal thank you card.

3. Set up a network of coordinators with sign out sheets for tokens; have an administrator monitor usage and redemption.

4. Never allow cash to be exchanged, either straight across or for change.

Step three: Select your recognition tools

Some examples of token usage include:

✓ Hotel

The hotel asked each customer to complete an input card on the different services it offered (maid service, valet parking, check-in/check-out, room service, bell service, etc.). If the highest possible rating was achieved, the group received a token to be accumulated for team awards and a team party. The purpose of this system was to achieve the best customer service possible.

✓ A major appliance store

The store solicited feedback on sales and service representatives during a follow-up phone call to customers. Any employee who received praise by the customer received a token. Tokens could be saved toward the purchase of anything in the store.

Gifts or Gift Certificates

A gift to thank someone for a positive behavior is a regular activity in our personal lives and can easily be translated into a work practice. Special merchandise can be ordered specific to your team effort, department, product, organization or corporation. These gifts might include a special logo item – T-shirt, jacket, pen, etc. – that notes the special activity. These gifts serve as a constant reminder, a keepsake of what the individual or team did to receive the recognition. Another option is to provide a variety of gift certificates, so that the person recognizing can select a certificate that fits the unique preferences of the recipient. For example, a fisherman or hunter might appreciate a gift certificate to a sporting goods catalog, a computer buff might appreciate a gift certificate to a media store, or a reader might appreciate a gift certificate to a book store. Remember, keep a variety of gift certificates as individual tastes widely vary.

134

Step three: Select your recognition tools

Pizza Party, Barbecue or Donuts

This is an easy and relatively simple way to reinforce a small group, such as a department, team or functional group, for accomplishing an identified milestone. It is relatively inexpensive, but, when combined with sincere appreciation from the beneficiaries of the effort and a mini-celebration, is very effective recognition.

Wall of Fame

Buy a few inexpensive cameras, some bulletin boards and distribute them throughout the company. Give the cameras to designated photographers, who become responsible for taking pictures of individuals and teams who have exemplified the principles and practices defined by the business goals during the last month. Accomplishments are visible to everyone and the individuals in the showcase become role models and are reinforced again for their contributions. Make sure you do not limit the number of people who can be shown on the wall of fame in a specific time period (i.e. employee of the month systems). The more, the merrier.

Publicity

Newsletters are a great way to reinforce individual and team accomplishments, as the people and their accomplishments are placed in the spotlight. You must ensure that the announcements are made close to the event to ensure the impact. Another clever publicity approach is to take an advertisement out in the local paper listing each individual's name and thanking the team members for their success (specifically call out the achievement).

Special Event Tickets

Award movie tickets or tickets to a sporting event, the theater or special city event. A special evening out creates a memorable occasion which the recipient will associate with his/her accomplishment.

Step three: Select your recognition tools

Traveling Trophy

The most famous of this type of award is Hewlett Packard's traveling "Golden Banana" award. In the UK, Reebok™ has one of their original athletic shoes floating around the company. A traveling trophy helps get every person involved in the recognition system. The person receiving the trophy has the responsibility of identifying the next recipient of the award. The award is usually designed to signify a specific behavior or accomplishment.

The Candy System

AIM Management Group, a very successful investment firm in Texas, developed a "candy system." Recipients may receive a variety of different "sweet rewards" such as:

- ✓ Lifesavers™ - comes with a note that says "Thanks for being a life saver today!"

- ✓ Nestle's Crunch Bar™ - comes with a note that say "Thanks for helping me through the crunch."

- ✓ Bar None™ - comes with a note telling the recipient why they were the greatest "bar none" that day.

The possibilities are endless with the numerous candy names you can work with and the investment is minimal.

Treasure Chest

Another method from AIM Management Group is a rolling treasure chest which the administrator rolls into the area, rings a loud bell and recognizes the recipient. In the chest, along with assorted pirate booty, is eight to twelve items with a value of approximately $20 each. There is logo merchandise, movie tickets, etc. The recipient is allowed to select whatever they would like. The gifts are changed frequently to maintain interest.

Time

Time off systems come in all shapes and varieties; we have even seen one that worked like "frequent flyer miles" with minutes building up over a long term. Often, time off with pay is more coveted than money. Other recognition systems which use time as the award include allowing employees to work different hours in the summer and flex time.

Special Dress Day

Special Dress Days are usually department events designed to let a business group celebrate achievement of a goal. By dressing unusually, they draw attention to themselves and when people ask "Why are you dressed like that?" - the employees earn bragging rights. There are many examples of special dress days including: casual day, shorts day, ugly T-shirt day, stripes day, purple day, most unusual hat day, 50s day, sports day, etc. Anything to draw attention to the employees celebrating.

Including the Employee's Family

A really nice touch is to write the employee's family to thank them when their family member has worked an extraordinary amount of time or to tell them how wonderful the employee's latest accomplishment is. One company sent an engineer's wife flowers when he had to be paged to come into work during a company special event.

Tools for Big Accomplishments

Tools for recognizing impact to the business goals and objectives are usually highly visible awards given with great fanfare and celebration. Again, the tools may be any nominal amount that fits your budget. This type of recognition is given for participating in an effort that realizes a measurable, sustained improvement which helps achieve a stated goal. Because this recognition is usually of a greater value, it generally requires the approval of the manager whose goals

Step three: Select your recognition tools

were reached from the effort (beneficiary). There are three things to remember when your require approval:

1) Always make the nomination process "short and sweet".

2) Continuously communicate that it is still everyone's responsibility to initiate recognition, even when the situation requires approval.

3) Management should never say "no" to a recognition opportunity.

To accomplish these objectives, ensure that you use a simple nomination form or process that concisely spells out the requirements (see example), so that when an individual or team is seeking recognition, it is clear. Train managers in the different recognition tools, so if a nomination does not merit a certain level of recognition, they can offer some reasonable alternatives to the nominator. In addition, provide everyone with a procedure that supports these decisions.

Example of a nomination form.

Step three: Select your recognition tools

INDIVIDUAL NOMINATION FORM
Mail to:
Recognition Process Administrator

This form is for individual "I Made a Difference" awards.
Complete all information. Thank you!!!

Date of Nomination

Information on Recipient

Name	Div/Dept	Mail	EXT.	Manager	Mail	EXT.

Nominator   Mail   Extension

Problem/Mission Statement

Brief description of individual's accomplishment

Desired measurable results (you may attach graphs)

Sponsoring Manager's Section
(To be completed by the sponsoring manager who realized benefit from this achievement)

❑ **Nomination form is complete and measurable results are attached.**
All sections have been completed and measurable results provided. This
individual completed a process improvement project making a SIGNIFICANT
CONTRIBUTION toward meeting or exceeding a department, organizational or
corporate goal established for a key business process. Measurable results
demonstrate the positive impact on the goals.

Signature of Sponsoring Manager

My signature verifies that this individual has satisfied the minimum requirement for the level of award.

Step three: Select your recognition tools

Here are some examples of higher level awards:

Team Excellence Celebration and Award

The Team Excellence Celebration and Award provides a means to recognize teams for their successes. Team Excellence requires a completed team nomination form (similar to the requirements shown on the Individual Nomination Form), the team mission statement, evidence of measurable results and the signature of the process owner (beneficiary of the improvement). The features of this award are the following: anyone can initiate it, the process is simple, and the nominees receive positive reinforcement in three ways. This award is designed for celebration and takes into consideration the importance of recognition from family, peers and management. The three positive reinforcements events are:

1) The immediate recognition is presented by the process owner. It includes a certificate identifying the specific contribution, a lapel pin specially designed for successful teams and a sincere verbal thank you.

2) The team is invited to a celebration, not to be confused with your typical company recognition banquets, luncheons or award ceremonies. The event is held during work hours. Each individual is allowed to bring one guest. This guest can be a co-worker, friend, family member – anyone the recipient chooses.

3) Each individual team member is allowed to select one award item from a list of eight to ten logo items, such as binoculars, garment bags, jackets, desk clocks, etc. The Team Excellence logo notes that they have actively participated in a successful team effort. These items are not for sale anywhere and can only be obtained through this achievement.

Some examples of measurable results might include:

140

Step three: Select your recognition tools

- ✓ Reduction in cycle time
- ✓ Reduction in defect rate
- ✓ Reduction in costs or expenses
- ✓ Development of a new process or new product
- ✓ Return on investment
- ✓ Reliability improvement
- ✓ Cost avoidance
- ✓ Reduction in labor hours
- ✓ Increase in customer or employee satisfaction indices.

Let's talk about celebration! The celebrations are not your typical award ceremonies which are stuffy and often overly formalized. They are held during work hours. They happen frequently during the year. They are limited to four or five teams per celebration to keep them small and personal. And most importantly, they are theme celebrations designed for fun. Use your imagination! Here are two examples of celebrations:

Celebration #1 - The Oscars

Clever and appropriately-designed invitations are mailed announcing the theme. Of course, all participants are fed. The room is decorated with top hats, glitter and chocolate Champagne bottles. Everyone in attendance knows in advance of the theme and are encouraged to dress for the occasion. Some show up in "tux look-alike" T-shirts, some wear furs and boas. Suddenly, the lights dim, the music starts and spotlights move rapidly across the audience. Jodie Foster and Hannibal the Cannibal (a man on a dolly in a straight jacket and restraining mask) impersonators walk (or roll) in to host the event. At this event, each team was allowed to nominate a person who was not a team member, but served as a vital support person during the project. These individuals have their accomplishments cited and are called forward to receive chocolate Oscars for "Best Supporting Actress or Actor". A team game is played in which each table tries to match the actors or actresses with the Academy Award winning film. The first team with a correct entry receives chocolate Champagne bottles and

141

movie tickets. Each team has a designated speaker who gives a five minute informal presentation on what the team accomplished and introduces each team member. At this time, each team member is congratulated by an upper level manager and given the award they selected previously. A motivational speaker is scheduled for a five minute speech to close the event and encourage the teams to keep up the good work.

Celebration #2 - The Fabulous Fifties.

This event follows the same agenda as Celebration #1, but saddle shoes, mouse ears and poodle skirts are the dress. Two Elvis impersonators entertain the crowd. The decorations are 45 rpm records, soda glasses, jukeboxes, 1950s model cars, etc. During lunch, the tunes of Connie Francis, Brenda Lee, Buddy Holly, Elvis and other 50s stars are played. Any individual who can produce a credit card with the numbers 1,9,5,0 in series receives a video tape rewinder that looks like a model '57 Chevy. Each table team is asked to reach consensus and guess the number of gumballs in a gum ball machine. The winning team gets 50s memorabilia. The team's designated speakers get officially inducted into the Mickey Mouse Club and receive their "ears." And so on . . .

The only standard items on the Team Excellence Celebration agenda are the team's five minute presentation, the guest speaker and a meal. From there, you can expect almost anything, making the event fun, exciting, always surprising – a celebration of success. Some other themes and highlights include:

✓ Luau – hula-hoop competition and name that Hawaiian tune.

✓ Olympics – game winners won gold medals (chocolate), were put on a pedestal and had the flag raised behind them to the National Anthem. An opening torch was lit. The team game was naming the countries of the flags decorating the room.

Step three: Select your recognition tools

✓ Fiesta – mariachis played. Sombreros with flowers decorated the tables. Carmen Miranda (impersonator) hosted the event. The team was identifying the prices of fast food items at Taco Bell™ – 59, 79 or 99.

There are hundreds of ideas to make these events experiences to remember.

The awards for the recipients are changed frequently to provide a variety and maintain interest level. All have the Team Excellence logo to provide a memory of the achievement for the recipient every time he/she looks at the item. If you are trying to promote the team approach to work, this is a perfect recognition tool.

Night on the Town

Another form of recognition is The Night on the Town. The Night on the Town is a type of recognition that provides an opportunity for employees to celebrate their exemplary work achievements with family and/or friends. It may be used to recognize an individual or a team. The immediate recognition is an attractive certificate noting the achievement which may be displayed. Again, anyone can nominate any individual or team for this award. The criteria is the same as for Team Excellence. Certificates can be made available throughout the company. To make it valid for exchange, the process owner must sign the certificate and indicate their division/department number. The stub on the certificate may be exchanged for a fine dining experience or for several gift certificates to family style restaurants.

This type of recognition is valuable to use for individual recognition and in those cases where a Team Excellence Celebration is not the choice of the recipients. Like the celebration, it allows the recipient the opportunity to share their work success with family and friends.

The "I Made a Difference" Award

This type of recognition is provided for the same type of contribution required by Team Excellence or the Night on the Town criteria. It is

Step three: Select your recognition tools

offered to those teams and individuals which might prefer a shopping spree and includes several options for gift certificates at local malls and through special mail order catalogs. The process for initiation and redemption is the same as for a Night on the Town.

Limousine Service

A great way to get an individual some peer attention is to get a limousine service to take the person to and from work for a week or to take the person and three friends out to lunch one day. Every one will sit up and take notice when they witness the employee being pampered.

Sport Cars

There are several car rental agencies which rent and lease expensive sports cars. Rent/lease one for a weekend to give an employee who has made a great contribution. Again, this is a very visible method of recognition.

Graduation Ceremony

After an employee completes a nominal amount of training (i.e. 100 hours), play "Pomp and Circumstance," give them a pseudo-diploma and bake them a cake. There are several other ways we can recognize our workforce. We can send them to special seminars and off-site training. Our executives can take people, who normally would not get to attend, to the big stockholders meeting, trade shows or sales meetings. Giving individuals special privileges, opportunities or responsibilities, although subtle, also translates into recognition. Remember, all recognition awards must include a show of sincere appreciation, acknowledgment and approval. You must make the experience special; give people something to talk about for years to come by making the experience dramatic, extraordinary and memorable.

Section 4:
MAGIC

*Work can provide the opportunity for spiritual
and personal, as well as financial, growth.
If it doesn't, then we're wasting too much
of our lives on it.*

James A. Autrey

Step four:

Show you care

"If an activity is not grounded in 'to love' or 'to learn,'
it does not have value."

Anne Rice

Guidelines for Delivering and Receiving Recognition

Nothing is more enjoyable than giving someone a gift or making someone feel special. It is equally rewarding for the giver and the recipient. Remember the seven criteria for effective recognition when delivering the recognition and

1.   **Be sincere.**

Nothing is worse than receiving appreciation or a gift from someone who really doesn't seem to care. Use your words, your body language and your token of appreciation to express *real* gratitude.

2.   **Be fair and consistent.**

Inequitable, inconsistent, undeserved or excessive recognition may be perceived as an insult, negating the positive results you want to achieve.

3.   **Be timely.**

An historical failure with recognition systems is that the recipient had to wait a year to receive recognition and the recognition process was weighed down with competitions, scoring and mounds of administration.

Step four: Show you care

The tools suggested previously provide for immediate recognition and the more immediate the recognition, the more likely you are to see the desired behavior or practice repeated.

4.   **Recognize frequently**.

Recognition should occur as often as the behaviors and practices are demonstrated. The Thanks system mentioned earlier can be applied liberally. Remember, the goal is to have recognition for everyone and to improve the quality of our work life and to help us achieve our business objectives more efficiently and effectively. This goal requires that recognition becomes part of our daily thoughts and work activity.

5.   **Be flexible.**

Spontaneous recognition should become the norm. The recognition processes in this book take very little time to initiate and allow for not only spontaneity, but creativity in making the recognition a personal statement from the giver.

6.   **Ensure the recognition is appropriate.**

Do not just recognize so often that the positive impact of recognition is lost in the flurry of activity. Devise a plan, defining what behaviors and practices are valuable to your business and how you will show appreciation on the occasions when the opportunity arises.

7.   **Be specific.**

Let the recipient know exactly what you are recognizing and the chances are history will repeat itself.

Step four: Show you care

Types of Acknowledgment

There are many ways to acknowledge contributions. Remember, always consider the feelings of the recipient. And, recognize with a method that is comfortable to you, so the message received is sincere, warm and heartfelt. Your plan for recognizing must fit your work culture and style.

Public or Private Acknowledgment

Public recognition should always be considered the preferred delivery method, as there is increased motivational value to both the receiver and the audience when attention is called to specific accomplishments. Public recognition has a much greater impact than recognition given privately.

If the recipient is particularly shy, embarrassed easily or very private, the giver should take into account these feelings and deliver the recognition one-on-one with little or no fanfare. Private recognition may also be the delivery method of choice when public recognition would elicit feelings of favoritism or undue competitiveness. These feelings can be avoided by establishing with your group the behaviors, goals and values you intend to recognize, asking everyone to watch for the identified actions and by encouraging everyone to be responsible for recognition.

The decision to give public or private recognition requires knowing the recipient, the recipient's peer environment and the presenter's own comfort level. As recognition becomes the rule instead of the exception in your workplace, public recognition should progress to where it is the norm, the chosen delivery method and accepted by everyone as a positive experience.

Formal or Informal Recognition

This decision is usually based on the magnitude of the accomplishment. In situations where the achievement commands considerable attention, the ceremonial quality and visibility

149

Step four: Show you care

afforded by formal recognition tends to be more appropriate. Again, some individuals may be very uncomfortable in a formal setting and their feelings should be considered. Recognition is evolving into the art of celebration, having fun and being in a comfortable situation.

<u>Verbal and/or Written Recognition</u>

A one-on-one verbal acknowledgment of a positive behavior or an exceptional accomplishment is the foundation to any recognition situation. When the behavior or accomplishment mainly affects the two parties, a sincere personal expression of acknowledgment and appreciation is the most appropriate. Prior to recognizing an individual or team in a peer environment, personal verbal recognition can ensure the proper amount of time is spent communicating the specific reason for the recognition to the recipient. There are several ways to facilitate verbal acknowledgment in the workplace including staff meetings, special meetings and an informal calling together of the peer group. The appropriate way to decide how the verbal recognition will be given is by determining what audience would most benefit from hearing about the accomplishment. Their recognition never should be given as an aside during a meeting. It should command special attention and include a statement of what the candidate did, why you consider it special and noteworthy, and how the activity helps the audience.

Documenting the recognition with a simple thank you or a more formal memo is a way to re-emphasize what you have shared verbally. It allows the giver to be personal and warm, and records the event to serve as a reminder or keepsake for the recipient. The document also allows the recipient to share the recognition with family, friends and co-workers. Written recognition can take many forms including a thank you note, a letter of commendation or an article in the company news. It is critical to remember, there is little or no value in a form letter with a stamped signature.

Step four: Show you care

<u>Double the Value</u>

The most valuable delivery method is to recognize using a verbal method reinforced with a written document, which is possible regardless of the type of award, setting selected or formality.

Receiving the Recognition

For some reason, our culture has conditioned us to deny or minimize compliments immediately. For instance, if someone says, "I love your dress!" you automatically reply, "This old thing! I got it for $30 on sale." Never is the compliment accepted at face value or affirmed by saying, "It is one of my favorites, too." We all need to learn to accept praise unconditionally and graciously. The act of recognizing takes a great deal of forethought and work. It is coming from the heart of the giver and often the recognition exchange is as important, valuable and exciting to the giver as it is to the receiver. Train yourself to be receptive to the giver and enjoy the benefits of feeling better about yourself and your work.

Be happy and celebrate!

Implementation tips

"The key word is 'creative.' Take the time to find out what
specifically motivates and excites each employee,
and then do your best to make those things happen.
Recognize accomplishments immediately in a
unique and memorable way."

Bob Nelson
"Secrets of Successful Employee Recognition"

Evolution Versus Revolution

PEOPLE do not like to have the "rug jerked out from under them." If you are revising your current recognition system, try an evolutionary approach. Plan the change with ease of acceptance in mind. Our evolutionary plan included the following strategies and tactics:

1. **Keep your current recognition tools as you introduce the new ones.**

   Even though the former recognition tools, $50 and $100 cash certificates, did not meet our criteria for effective recognition, we continued to provide these awards. By doing this, we avoided the perception that something was being taken away. These old systems of recognition, over a period of three years significantly decreased in use from lack of interest and because they required so much bureaucratic nonsense. As people became familiar with the new tools, which included the "caring and sharing" and more personal touches, they became the tools of choice.

2. **Pilot the tools one at a time in a small section of your corporation.**

We piloted our thanks cards combined with tokens in an organization of 1800 people (approximately 20% of our corporate population). We followed later with Team Excellence and Night on the Town awards. In this way, we started with the needs of the majority first. "Thanks" was only in place for three months when other organizations began requesting participation. By conducting pilots, you can collect data on costs and employee satisfaction to provide to those organizations less likely to take a risk without more information. This also provides the opportunity to fine-tune the system before wider deployment.

3. **Measure each tool for employee satisfaction and make improvements continuously.**

Many of our measurements are collected in-process. For example, surveys collected from a random sample of Team Excellence participants have results plotted on a control chart. One control chart showed the rating on the meal went "out of control" after one celebration. The menu was changed prior to the next celebration bringing our process back into control. By monitoring eight different attributes of the celebration process, we can stay on top of recipient needs.

4. **Charter a cross-functional team to select awards, roll out new tools, track and improve processes, and plan celebrations.**
A management assumption during our development phase was that engineers, assemblers, managers, consultants, accountants and administrative associates would not all respond to the same recognition system,

that some professions would only respond to cash and high value awards. We have no hard data to support this assumption. Everyone likes to feel appreciated and the gift is definitely not the focus – "It's the thought that counts!" In order to address this concern, we created a cross-functional recognition council. This council functions as a steering committee and has one representative from each functional organization.

5.   **Ensure that management is well-versed in the recognition philosophy and tools.**

We began by giving management overviews. Changing the old environment of authority (telling people what to do and disciplining them when they don't) to an environment of positive reinforcement does not happen overnight. James A. Autrey, in *Love and Profit*, states,

> *"It's the old story of managers who fancy that their job is police work rather than missionary work. They become so preoccupied with making sure their employees are not doing the wrong thing that they fail to recognize the right thing, which may be something not according to the rules."*

Remember, managers are human beings too and need positive reinforcement to drive their performance changes. To help facilitate the transformation, it is important not only to train management in the recognition philosophy and tools, but to give them a goal related to recognition and motivating employees, eliminate any negative consequences and positively reinforce them for making the performance change.

Since anyone can initiate the recognition tools,

you need to train all of the workforce. Whenever you empower people and give them new responsibilities, it is critical to train the managers for "handing over the baton". To encourage the entire workforce to accept this new responsibility, we asked managers to serve as role models and actively participate in the recognition processes. We also gained their agreement to guide their reports in proper use of the tools and to allow them to participate in recognition training.

6. **Produce and distribute a procedure manual to every employee.**

All recognition methods had process flowcharts and accompanying procedures. It was critical that recognition be considered a work process, no different than any other work process. This manual helped reinforce the fact that recognition was not an "extra" or a "nice gesture." Each recognition process was continuously improved using the corporation's standardized quality improvement process. By distributing to every employee, we reinforced the concept that recognition is everyone's responsibility.

7. **Select a high-level sponsor.**

It is critical to find a true believer in the upper layers of management who will run interference for your efforts and secure the necessary resources. At one point, we almost lost part of our system due to a budget cut directive. Our sponsor prevented this catastrophe. In addition, he hired a full-time recognition process administrator to maintain the system. This further validated the importance of recognition in the workplace. Oddly enough, our original sponsor was the vice-president of manufacturing, not the person or function you would guess would take responsibility for the recogni-

Implementation tips

tion processes. This turned out to be a blessing in disguise. It was the largest organization, placing the recognition support where it would be most visible. It was isolated from the "reward" function, so recognition finally gained the focus it rightfully deserved. Finally, it kept recognition out of the corporate bureaucracy that might threaten the simplicity and availability of the tools. It was a total paradigm shift and a major risk that paid off for all functional organizations. Only through the belief and people-oriented management style of our sponsor, did the system achieve its full potential.

8.   Establish a recognition network.

Walt Disney once said *"Many hands, hearts and minds generally contribute to anyone's notable achievements."* One person could not make these processes work. Not even ten people could. We began by soliciting one volunteer from each department to work on recognition. We gave each individual special holders for thank you cards, a supply of thank you cards and envelopes, and some tokens. We explained the importance of their role in starting and maintaining the process. We followed with regular one-on-one communication and a big annual meeting where the volunteers were given a gift of appreciation and introduced to what's up and coming in recognition. Another critical part of the recognition network is the co ordination department and purchasing agent. We worked very hard to develop agreements that were mutually beneficial and guaranteed long-term partnerships. Finally, we worked to establish a partnership with management, specifically those managers who would actively support and participate in the recognition process, and provide the motivation and momentum to keep the processes focused. The entire network consists of approximately

157

150 people (in a company of 6000) or 1.5% of the company's employees. These individuals are instrumental to sustaining the recognition effort.

9.   Address management's concern on "abuse".

Part of management's concern prior to the pilot was that the systems would be abused. In their minds, abuse = overuse, friends collaborating for fun and profit. It turned out that in eight years, only once did such collusion occur. It probably cost more to track the system than it did to cover the abuse! The tracking did reveal another type of abuse – lack of use. Our goal was to recognize 100% of the employee population on an annual basis. When lack of use was identified, we gave personal presentations to the identified departments and devised ways to somehow thank them or involve them in a recognition event.

10.   Provide a clear tie to your corporation's quality initiatives.

We had a TQM initiative that called out recognition as the ninth step of a standardized quality improvement process. On introducing the recognition process, everyone was given a mug imprinted with this process on the side. Recognition was in bold print. Employees were encouraged to use the process to reduce costs, improve quality or reduce cycle time and to use the new recognition process to celebrate success.

You can tie your recognition system to any new initiative; the greatest value add comes from recognizing individual performance and team success to your business goals. Create a matrix showing how goals relate to the recognition system.

11.   Budget at a high level.

Implementation tips

You can budget any amount you wish to invest on recognition awards. Again, it is the attention and the thought that counts. Our first system budgeted $100 per employee, not including service awards. Our system was budgeted at the vice-presidential level for the following several reasons

✓ To reduce management fear, resistance to change and cutbacks incorporated to achieve favorable budget variances. Usage by individual manager or department is invisible on management reports. This eliminates the risk of "robbing Peter to pay Paul" in individual department budgets. There is no risk of designated funds being used accidentally or intentionally for another or the wrong purpose.

✓ To demonstrate commitment to recognition. The money is in a special recognition budget; the amount has been committed and can only be used for recognition. The recognition administrator maintains and monitors the use. Both management and non-management perceive this as upper-level management commitment, ensuring that the tool will be used consistently.

✓ To simplify administration. Only a handful of budgets need to be monitored and maintained versus hundreds. In an average size corporation, this entails five to ten budgets at the executive vice-president level. If all managers had budgets, the total would rise to 200+.

✓ To limit the reporting requirements. As

159

mentioned previously, when only a handful of budgets are affected, the set of management reporting requirements and expectations is kept to a minimum. This prevents the recognition administrator from becoming a "slave to many masters". Information is given at the staff meetings of the involved vice-presidents, who are then responsible to disseminate the information down through the management ranks.

These strategies and tactics provided us with the foundation for successful implementation and for making recognition a part of daily work activities. "Slow, but sure" and "dramatic, not drastic" were our mottoes. Within three years, the system was fully operational throughout the corporation. Within eight years, the percentage of employee population recognized rose from 1.6% to 94%.

These implementation tips will help ensure that your system is truly designed for the employee, to meet their specific needs. It also addresses the resistance to change issues encountered by any new philosophy or change in work processes. In addition, measurements can be used to convince skeptics who follow the old school of management style, those who believe any accomplishment is "just their job", and that the only effective forms of recognition involve competition, contests, judging, a formal banquet and winners.

The magician

"He is the best leader who most fully understands the nature of things,
so that his plans are not doomed to ultimate failure;
who possesses an active, far-ranging imagination
which can see many possibilities;
who has a sense of values,
so that among possibilities he is able to choose the most excellent;
who has a sense of order,
to give form, design and program to the values and purposes he selects;
who has practical sense and judgment,
and so uses the most feasible means to accomplish his ends;
and who has the energy and enthusiasm
to carry his plans persistently toward fruition."

Arthur E. Morgan

THE most important part of your implementation strategy is selecting your administrator. You will definitely need at least one person who exclusively works on recognition administration. As in the quote above, this person must be persistent, imaginative, intuitive, principled, organized, practical, energetic and enthusiastic. The individual **must** be a "people person", respected by management, knowledgeable in diversity, and well-liked and considered approachable by the general population. Listening and communication skills are required. The tasks are many, but the job is personally rewarding. Some of the administrator's responsibilities include marketing,

The magician

"adminis-trivia," consulting, purchasing, accounting, benchmarking, process maintenance, management reporting and event facilitation. Quite a list! Some of the related tasks are:

Marketing

- ✓ Identifying areas of low usage and encouraging participation.
- ✓ Regular presentations at all employee meetings.
- ✓ News articles on success stories for company newsletters.

"Adminis-trivia"

- ✓ Creating and mailing invitations.
- ✓ Designing and producing special certificates.
- ✓ Response to requests by E-mail, phone, FAX and mail.
- ✓ Screening forms for data pertinent to management reports and publicity.
- ✓ Scheduling special events for teams.
- ✓ Keeping the recognition network informed.

Consulting

- ✓ Helping in management decisions regarding the type of recognition.
- ✓ Chairing a cross-functional team responsible for maintaining recognition processes.
- ✓ Answering questions.
- ✓ Serving as resident expert on recognition.
- ✓ Staying current on the latest and greatest industry best practices in recognition.
- ✓ Providing ideas on how to recognize specific individuals and specific contributions.

Purchasing

- ✓ Working with suppliers to get samples of new awards.
- ✓ Setting up purchase orders.
- ✓ Maintaining a supply of gift certificates and gifts.
- ✓ Taking care of "special orders".

Accounting

- ✓ Maintaining the recognition budget.
- ✓ Charging appropriate accounts for funds used.
- ✓ Ensuring there is ample funding for celebrations, awards and supplies.

Benchmarking

- ✓ Responding to external requests for information on the system.
- ✓ Continuous external research for ideas to enhance the system.

Process Maintenance

- ✓ Maintaining supplies such as thank you cards, certificates, gifts, etc.
- ✓ Working with creative design on logos.
- ✓ Maintaining award inventory.
- ✓ Rolling out new improvements to the processes.
- ✓ Updating the procedure manual.

Management Reporting

- ✓ Monthly management reporting on cost per employee, preferred tools, number of individuals and teams recognized, etc.
- ✓ Identifying areas which are not using the recognition tools and those with success stories.

The magician

Event Facilitation

- ✓ Conducting team events.
- ✓ Working to set up times and places for celebrations.
- ✓ Helping to decorate for special events.
- ✓ Ensuring that awards and certificates are at the right place at the right time.

This is just a partial list. As you can see, this position requires someone with a great disposition, a sense of humor and the ability to communicate well, both in writing and verbally to management and non-management. The most important quality for the administrator is that they are honest, approachable and personable. They should represent everything that is "good," as their job is positive reinforcement. Appointing a special administrator for recognition sends a message to the workforce that management is serious about recognition. It is not an extra job for someone to pick up, not if you are committed to changing the way you operate your business. And, it is not a job that just any person can assume.

Where should the administrator report? The original system we worked in was sponsored by the VP of manufacturing, so the administrator reported to him. Even after the tools and processes were deployed throughout the corporation, it was decided to keep this arrangement. The reasons behind this decision included:

1) You would never think of having the manufacturing organization in charge of recognition; the manufacturing organization had the greatest percentage of the population, so this reinforced the philosophy that recognition was everyone's responsibility, not just a management job or a task for the human resource's function. Also, recognition was supported by a cross-functional team, so why should it matter who the administrator reports to?

164

2) This allowed for thinking outside of our paradigm. The normal functional organizations responsible for recognition would never have the new perspectives and new ideas gained from this effort. This allowed for thinking "outside the box" and great changes.

3) When administered by a corporate service function, all of the sudden recognition becomes impersonal – a corporate strategy – a budget to be cut and an administrative nightmare. Keep recognition as close to the individual as possible. Drive it to the first line.

Step five:
Measure, monitor
and continuously improve
your recognition processes

*"For managers, the most important job is not measurement
but motivation and you can't motivate numbers."*

James A. Autrey

THE greatest recognition mistake in our businesses is treating recognition as a benefit instead of a work process. This paradigm will not continue if we treat recognition like our most important work processes. How do we handle our most important processes? We create flowcharts or step-by-step instructions, we train and certify our workforce, we establish goals and monitor performance, and so forth. Effective recognition is our most valuable work process; it is the only process that can positively impact every corporate goal and attribute revenue, cycle time, quality, etc. You must use the same plan, do, check and act strategy that you apply on other business processes.

Whenever a change is implemented, a multitude of measurements are collected to ensure the validity of the new approach and to convince the skeptics to join forces with the rest of the team. This system is no different. In fact, there is a management paradigm that recognition is on the softer side of leadership and work skills, causing the system to come under greater scrutiny and suspicion, and requiring even more evidence of effectiveness. Management had several measurement requirements for the pilot effort of this system to initiate recognition; they were fully cognizant that our personal goal was for the system to recognize 100% of the population versus the less than 2% that were recognized by the former system. The proposal involved a great risk in their minds, both to the budget and management discretion and power. The mandated management measurements at start-up included:

- ✓ Usage

  How much are we spending, on what, where and with which tool?

- ✓ Abuse

  Who is over-using the privilege?

- ✓ Costs

  How much is this costing us per person?

Our mission clearly needed data on other system attributes collected. We had specific challenges to meet if the system was to be deemed "effective" in our eyes, including:

- ✓ A steady increase in the percentage of the population recognized with a goal of 100%.

- ✓ The ability to determine which tools were meaningful and well-received.

- ✓ To ensure that the recognition included those who were important to the recipient, whether it be management, family, friends or co-workers.

Step five: Measure, monitor and continuously improve your recognition processes

✓   To verify the timeliness of each tool.

✓   To have evidence that the deployment of the methods had reached all departments and areas.

To establish an effective measurement system, we took both the management requirements and the goals established from our mission and determined the answers to the following questions:

1.   What information and data do we need to collect? What questions do we need answered?

2.   What decisions will we make from this data and information?

3.   What format should we use to present the data?

4.   How often should the data be reported?

5.   How will we monitor the process?

6.   What "signals" will we react to?

7.   How will problems and improvement opportunities be identified and prioritized?

8.   How will we ensure that the employees are motivated and satisfied?

Management requirements were met by tracking dollars spent per employee, sorted by the functional organization. This data collection addressed the need to know cost, usage and possible abuse. The purpose of the recognition team was met by identifying the critical success factors of each tool and collecting surveys on the factors. Surveys were given to a random sample of employees immediately after they received their recognition. The scale was one to seven and all data was plotted on control charts to closely monitor the processes.

Potential benefits of effective recognition systems

"People work for self-expression. Even when they talk loudest about 'getting the money,' they are really most interested in doing a job skillfully, so that others will admire it and give them that inward glow of satisfaction which comes of achievement. From the painter, producing his masterpieces, to the truck driver, piloting his leviathan across city streets, the basic inward thought is: 'I am the best caballero in all Mexico.'"

Howard Vincent O'Brien

THE benefits from providing good methods and practices for recognition in the workplace are extensive. They are comparable to the benefits of any positive reinforcement you have seen applied and are an invaluable tool to teach new behaviors or change existing ones. The fast pace and volatility of the marketplace demands we have the ability to change dramatically and learn quickly.

As you can see by the following list of benefits, recognition can be the critical instrument to facilitate this learning. Using recognition effectively and appropriately:

Potential benefits of effective recognition systems

- Drives performance improvement in every measurable corporate attribute.

- Drives individual and team performance improvement.

- Reinforces desired behaviors, practices, principles and values.

- Gives us a mechanism to show appreciation and say "thanks!"

- Builds self-esteem and morale.

- Promotes trust and respect.

- Fosters change.

- Celebrates success.

- Improves the quality of work life.

- Motivates individuals and teams to do their best.

- Enhances loyalty.

- Creates a positive attitude and confidence that carries to dealings with customers and suppliers.

- Addresses the basic human need to feel appreciated.

- Reflects commitment to others in our organization; helps establish superior relationships.

- Inspires accomplishment and achievement.

- Empowers individuals and teams.

Potential benefits of effective recognition systems

- Encourages teamwork.

- Builds faith.

- Drives out fear.

- Impacts the bottom line positively.

CLOSING THOUGHTS

If you will pay attention, listen, be accessible, open up, and provide your people with as many special treatments and celebrations and learning experiences as you can, you'll be overwhelmed by the abundance of rich thinking all around you.

James A. Autrey

"Caring"

*"If you don't CARE about people, get out of management
before it's too late."*

*"Those workers want to know how much you CARE before they
care how much you know."*

*"The objective is not to get everyone to love each other, only to CARE
about each other in the context of their work lives."*

James A. Autrey
Love and Profit

THERE has been much speculation about the decline of American
business during the second half of the twentieth century. All kinds
of theories, quality philosophies and practices, and consultants rose
from this upheaval. Most of these programs and processes were
good, from SPC to JIT. But, tools are only as good as the individual
or group applying them. We lost in the marketplace when we
stopped caring – caring about the quality of our products and
services, caring about our employees, caring about our co-workers
and caring about our customers and suppliers. We took these relationships for granted and withheld our attention and appreciation.
We became superficial and automatic in our dealings and communications. We concentrated on the almighty buck. We were wrong!

"Caring"

Pride in workmanship cannot be measured on a control chart. Creativity and innovation are not identifiable in a design of experiments. Honesty, sincerity and manners cannot be delivered in a box. Yet all of these personal qualities are necessary to operate competitively and successfully, and are necessary if our businesses are to survive into the millennium.

Many times, our managers are compared to parents. But, this analogy is drawn from their disciplinary and authority role in the workplace. I have had a manager tell me "I did it for your own good. You'll thank me later!" – sounding suspiciously like my father. To tell the truth, I often refer to one manager as my "Denver dad". Disciplining should be an infrequent activity; our time should not be spent trying to catch someone doing something wrong. I would like to see this "parental" image in a new light, one where managers truly care about their people.

I recently had a child graduate from high school. Of course, I cried with pride and joy. This event caused me to reflect on the past 18 years and everything I had done to facilitate this moment. I had provided a safe and secure environment; I had ensured the proper training and education; I had provided the tools and equipment needed, everything from the current "right" athletic shoes to pencils, pens and notebooks; I had set the rules and helped with the goals; I had listened to and shared in dreams, difficulties and disappointments; I helped through sickness, stitches and suffering through personal issues; I applauded and celebrated victories and offered kind words to refocus during defeats; I was always there and I always cared; I accepted my child for what he was, not forcing upon him my expectations of what I wanted him to be. This is exactly the kind of caring we need in the workplace. We need a safe and secure environment, and leaders that provide us with training, tools, rules, goals, and open ears. We need leaders that applaud and celebrate our positive accomplishments, and help us regroup when we fail or suffer defeat. We need leaders that accept us as unique individuals with unique gifts and unique needs. Being a parent is so much more than being a disciplinarian. Just like real parents, we need managers that care about us as human beings, not as employee numbers, head count (which is the number of steers in the cattle drive), dollar signs

178

in the labor/overhead column or, the worst term of all, "human resources" which makes us sound like they can order us up from the same catalog they buy equipment and tools from.

There is definitely a difference between our performance when we "have to" do a job and when we "want to" do the work. The difference is measurable on any scale. The difference between these two states of effort is the difference between "minimum possible" and "maximum ever." It is the difference between "I don't care!" and "I really care." And, this incredible difference in performance can result from the effective use of recognition in the workplace.

My second favorite question – right after "When do I say thank you?" – is "What is the ROI (return on investment) realized from an effective recognition system?" My answer is "How much is it costing you not to have a recognition system?" What would happen tomorrow if you went into work and suddenly every person (even that 70-90% that are doing just enough to get by) was working to their full potential? Every one would probably have their work completed before the first coffee break, you would have to sell some of your ideas to another manufacturer because you had too many to ever produce and there wouldn't be any problems before long, only opportunities. WOW! What would I pay for that? Let's consider some of the potential gains of "caring":

Caring about the quality of our work

- Improved sales
- Increased revenues
- Higher stock price
- Better marketplace position.

Caring about our employees

- Improved performance
- Lower attrition rate
- Less stress-related illnesses
- Fewer attendance problems
- Increased company pride; employees that go to

"Caring"

other companies to brag and share their success stories, not to turn in their resumes

- Improved morale and quality of work life
- More effort from employees to go the extra mile, to be creative, to reach goals.

Caring about our peers

- Improved teamwork
- Improved communication
- Elimination of barriers, both functional and performance-related
- Improved work environment
- Less competition and sabotage.

Caring about customers

- Drives repeat business
- Improved satisfaction levels
- Can be deciding factor for selecting supplier, if prices and services are comparable
- Can determine survival.

Caring about suppliers

- Long-term partnerships
- Improved performance
- Can gain priority service
- Reduction in supplier base.

Most all of these items add dollars to the bottom line of the balance sheet. And what about the other side of the coin? What are the disadvantages to "caring"?

Zero.

We have all kinds of consultants and initiatives to drive

180

change, resolve problems and continuously improve. Every one of them makes some kind of promise either to decrease costs, or reduce cycle time or improve our product/service. But, a dramatic culture change is required to successfully integrate and gain the greatest benefit from these initiatives. Approaching our work systematically and improving our service and products continuously requires a fundamental change in our *modus operandi*. Like any other change, it will require a well-thought out strategy and planning. There are two critical considerations or change agents necessary to drive such a transformation – first, you have to care and then, you need knowledge of reinforcement so that you can demonstrate "caring" effectively. All kinds of complicated ways can be developed to fulfill this requirement. It is really quite simple to drive change – eliminate the negative consequences and have positive consequences ready to encourage the change. ALL CHANGE AND LEARNING IS THE RESULT OF REINFORCEMENT!

"It is more blessed to give than to receive."

Acknowledgements

THIS book is the result of nine years of research, experience and networking. During this time, we have had so many supporters – family, friends, co-workers, clients and suppliers – that is really difficult to narrow the field to a short list of people to acknowledge. We would like to thank all of you from the bottom of our hearts. We would also like to thank those who have called, sent us books and articles, written letters, listened to our presentations, served as our role models and published our materials. And, we would not be able to spread our message without our clients and readers. Every single person we have met on this journey has had an impact on our philosophy and this book. We are sure you can see your influence.

To practice what we preach, however, we would like to thank those individuals who are a daily source of strength and support, and who are living examples of our beliefs.

Our Families

Jim Glasscock

You are a great husband. You continue to serve as an inspiration to Kim and I. We both appreciate the countless hours of free labor you provide on the behind-the-scenes activities that help to make our business manageable and successful. I gratefully acknowledge and express my deepest appreciation for the extra-mile support you always willingly and unfailingly provide to me. Thank you, Jim, for your constant love, interest and insight, Sue

Gene Stefanski

You are my best friend. You provided me with a living example of how treating people right and showing sincere appreciation pays off professionally and personally. I am really thankful for your advice on work scenarios, true service, personal improvement and motivating volunteers. Your feedback greatly enhanced this book. You are a role model of how the highest personal values can be integrated into our work lives. My thanks and greatest love and admiration. Kim.

Dustin, Jessica, Todd, Beau, Kelly and Tyler

You have given us loads of background material and experience on the power of reinforcement. Your never-ending patience with our travel and our schedules has been beyond comparison. Thank you for your devotion and daily demonstrations of love, Kim and Sue

Jack and Peggy Gram and Leon and Helen Shafer

As our parents, you have been our source of many lessons on unconditional love. Your support has made the difference in our lives. We know that you provided the foundation for our success today. Thank you for your pride that gave us the confidence to pursue our dream, Kim and Sue

Sarah B. Johnson

You are more than a niece, you are a wonderful person. Thanks for bringing me research material. I didn't even have to ask. You heard about our newest project and showed up the next day with materials you thought would help. Thanks for the help, Sue

Our Special Friends

Robb Farquhar

You captured our thoughts in pictures. We know how difficult it must be for an artist to express personal feelings that are not his own. You have so many extraordinary gifts – your artistic ability, your listening skills, your positive approach to feedback and your special way of understanding people. Thanks for sharing your talent with us, Kim and Sue

Debbra Griggs, Judd Meyers and Dick Ralston

During my career at StorageTek, I would have to say the three of you had the greatest influence on me. You allowed me to take risks, even when you might suffer the backlash; you encouraged me to pursue my education and gave me books to read, even though the smarter I got, the more dangerous I became; you challenged me to new performance levels, giving me several doses of my own reinforcement "medicine". All of you are exemplary of the term "leadership".Thanks, I love you all, Kim

Scott Miller

I have been fortunate to have a "true" partnership with you and your company – Boise Marketing Services, Inc., Denver. As general manager and my supplier, you have demonstrated the values I most appreciate in a customer/supplier relationship – honesty, integrity, respect and genuine concern for others. Thanks for the support and going the extra mile that helped make my celebrations a success, Sue

God

Without our faith, our lives and work would not have meaning. We thank you, God, for being our strength always, our help in the present and our hope for the future. We know, without You, we would not have completed our work and spread our message successfully.

Books cited and recommended

WE would highly recommend the following reading for those interested in recognition. We have used all of these books in our research. In our opinions, these authors are the most insightful and informative in their individual fields of expertise, accurately identifying the skills and actions required of leaders if their businesses are to be successful into the millennium. The list, alphabetical by author is :

Robin Ahert, Eliot Aronsen, Timothy Wilson
Social Psychology (second edition)

James A. Autrey
Love and Profit

Jan Carlzon
Moments of Truth

Bill Catlette & Richard Hadden
Contented Cows Give Better Milk

James C. Collins and Jerry L. Porras
Built to Last - Successful Habits of Visionary Companies

Covey Leadership Center
"The Habit of Communication"

Stephen Covey
Seven Habits of Highly Effective People

Bibliography

Aubrey C. Daniels
Bringing Out the Best In People

Aubrey C. Daniels
Performance Management: Improving Quality Productivity Through Positive Reinforcement

Sue Glasscock & Kimberly Gram
Saying Thanks

Gary Hamel Business Week, 5/5/97
Online Interview

Gary Hamel & C.K. Prahalad
Competing for the Future

Gary Heil, Tom Parker & Deborah C. Stephens
One Size Fits One

John Naisbitt
Megatrends

Carla O'Dell
People, Performance and Pay

Claire Raines
Beyond Generation X

John Marshall Reeve
Understanding Motivation and Emotion

INDEX

A

abuse concerns,	**160, 170**
accepting praise,	**153**
acknowledgements,	**20, 43-44, 185-187**
administrator,	**163-167**
AIM Management Group,	**117, 136**
Air Force Academy,	**115**
alignment	
definition,	**109-110**
process of,	**109-112**
American Compensation Association, quoted,	**60**
American Productivity and Quality Center, quoted,	**89**
American Psycholinguistic Society,	**76**
appreciation,	**16, 20, 41, 43-44**
appropriateness,	**55-56, 150**
approval,	**20, 43-44**
attention welcomed,	**98**
attrition rates,	**29-31**
automatic rewards,	**104**
Autrey, James A, quoted,	**107, 125, 147, 157, 169, 177, 179**
awards selection,	**156-157**

B

baseline survey,	**35-40**
behavior	
analysis,	**118-119**
changes,	**75**
codes,	**25**
consequence determines,	**79**
definition,	**71**
reinforcing,	**19-20**
understanding,	**78-79**
benefits package,	**105**

Index

benefits, potential,	**173-174**
Berra, Yogi, quoted,	**35**
bibliography,	**188-189**
body language,	**14**
Bojaxhiu, Agnes Gonxha see Teresa, Mother	
Bonvicini, Candido, quoted,	**65**
bragging rights,	**137**
Brokaw, Tom, quoted,	**59**
Brown, Mark Graham, quoted,	**110**
budget control,	**161-162**
Buscaglia, Leo, quoted,	**97**
Business Week, quoted,	**19**

C

Cameron, Julia, quoted,	**43**
candy system,	**136**
caring,	**30, 179-183**
Carlzon, Jan, quoted,	**30-31, 71**
Carnegie, Andrew, quoted,	**105**
cash	
not a motivator,	**86, 89**
recognition,	**84**
shifts focus,	**85**
Catlette, Bill, quoted,	**55, 88**
celebrations,	**16, 40, 102, 141-143**
change	
driving,	**12, 20**
examples,	**22-23**
human expertise,	**24**
ineffective,	**22-23**
management of,	**22**
resistance to,	**21-22**
characteristics of recognition systems,	**132**
charts	
behaviors, actions and milestones,	**119**
recognition and reward,	**62**
Collins, James C, quoted,	**25**
communications	
body language,	**14**
definition,	**13**
excitement for work,	**26**
improving,	**13-15**
in-person,	**14**

negative,	**17-18**
tone,	**14**
words,	**14**
competition	
cost of internal,	**92**
definition,	**91**
demotivation,	**94**
employee of the month,	**95**
environment,	**91**
focus on the award,	**93**
intense within organisations,	**92**
losers outnumber winners,	**94**
politics,	**93-94**
reasons to eliminate,	**92-95**
relationship problems,	**93**
salesperson of the year,	**95**
same people win,	**97**
consistency,	**46-48, 149**
cost containment	
employee retention,	**29-31**
non-monetary awards,	**61**
Covey, Stephen, quoted,	**15**
cross-functional recognition council,	**157**
culture of company,	**32-33**
customer: definition,	**18**
customers	
definition,	**18**
expectations,	**19**
goals,	**111**
impact of employees,	**27**
loyalty,	**18**
unhappy,	**17-18**
cynicism,	**19**

D

Daniels, Aubrey C	
beliefs,	**79**
quoted,	**21, 23,-24, 48, 66, 72, 75, 76, 79, 87, 87,-88, 115**
deadlines,	**93**
definitions	
alignment,	**109-110**
behaviorism,	**71**
communication,	**13**
competition,	**91**

Index

customer,	18
recognition,	43
relationship,	17
reward,	59-60
Deming, W Edwards, quoted,	61
demotivative effect,	94
discretionary effort,	83
Disney, Walt, quoted,	159
documenting recognition,	152-153

E

effectiveness criteria,	104, 149-151
emotions of recognition,	16
employee of the month,	121-122
employees	
as customers,	15
as volunteers,	16
asset of,	30-31, 32
bragging rights,	137
burnt-out,	31
engagement in work,	31
impact on customers,	27
loyalty,	29
motivation,	46
needs,	180
obligation to,	25
potential of,	31-32
recognition preferences,	39
rusted-out,	31
salary dissatisfaction,	91
valuable asset,	30-31, 32
employer loyalty,	29
evolutionary approach,	155
examples	
anniversaries,	42-44
appropriate to circumstances,	55-56
cash awards,	28
children,	75, 180
Christmas gifts,	51-52
family rewards,	56
gradual goals,	113-114
impossible goals,	112-113
ineffective change,	22-23
management failings,	73-75

negative feedback,	73
pay does not lead to results,	88-90
project completion,	27
reduction in force,	73
reinforcing the wrong thing,	121-125
specific rewards,	57
suggestion systems,	47-48
team awards,	28, 52-53, 124
timing,	49-50
varying rewards,	54-55
excitement for work,	26
expectations and performance,	98-99
extinction,	71, 72
eye contact,	14

F

fairness,	46-48, 149
family inclusion,	137
Farquhar, Robb,	187
fear management,	71
flexibility,	54,-55, 129, 150
Flowers, Dr Betty Sue, quoted,	94
Forehand, Larry, quoted,	30
formal recognition,	152
forms	
Individual Nomination form,	139
Recognition Survey,	36-40
frequency,	51-53, 150
Frost, Robert, quoted,	20
funny money,	133-134
future rewards,	79

G

gas stations,	17
Gebhardt, Joan, quoted,	49
Ghandi, Mohandas, quoted,	20
gifts or gift certificates,	134
Glanz, Barbara, quoted,	54
Glasscock, Jim,	185
goals	
achievement,	40
annual,	112-113

193

Index

cascading,	**110, 114**
continuous process,	**114-115**
cost,	**110**
cultural,	**111**
customer,	**111**
employee,	**111**
facts,	**114-115**
gradual,	**113-114**
impossible,	**112-113**
inspirational,	**112**
meaningful,	**114**
measurable,	**115**
milestones,	**53**
myths,	**112-114**
numerous,	**114**
quality,	**111**
same for all,	**113-114**
short-term,	**69**
timeliness,	**111**
verbal contracts,	**115**
visibility,	**115**
graduation ceremony,	**144**
Graham, Gerald, quoted,	**89**
Gram, Jack and Peggy,	**186**
Griggs, Debbra,	**187**

H

Haas, Robert, quoted,	**46**
Hadden, Richard, quoted,	**55, 88**
Hamel, Gary, quoted,	**19, 87**
Hawthorne effect,	**26, 98**
Heil, Gary, quoted,	**15, 26, 27, 29, 30, 32, 44, 86, 92, 117**
Herzberg, Frederick	
beliefs,	**77-78**
quoted,	**77-78, 89, 109**
Hewlett Packard,	**136**

I

I made a difference award,	**143-144**
ideas discredited,	**74-75**
immediacy,	**49-50**
implementing a recognition system,	**155-162**

Index

Individual Nomination form,	**141**
informal recognition,	**154**
Inventure Group,	**31**
It is not the gift, it's the thought that counts,	**21, 46**

J

James, William, quoted,	**41**
Jefferson, Thomas, quoted,	**83**
job security,	**29**
Johnson, Rheta Grimsley, quoted,	**13**
Johnson, Sarah B,	**186**

K

Kettering, Charles, quoted,	**77**
King, Rev Martin Luther Jr, quoted,	**24, 81**
KITA,	**77**

L

Lamont Corporation,	**31**
leadership	
skills,	**26**
style,	**44**
limousine service,	**144**
losers,	**93**
lottery,	**101**
louder, longer, meaner method,	**23**
loyalty,	**15, 18, 24, 26, 29, 123-124**

M

MacGregor, Douglas,	**78**
management	
biggest mistakes,	**89**
failings,	**73-75**
skills,	**26**
style,	**44**
training,	**157-158**
management by objectives,	**74**
Maslow, Abraham	

195

Index

beliefs,	**77, 90**
quoted,	**77**
Mayo, Elton, quoted,	**88**
McAdams, Jerry, quoted,	**60, 61**
Mead, Margaret, quoted,	**11**
measuring recognition process,	**169-171**
measuring results,	**156**
Meyers, Judd,	**187**
milestones,	**40, 53, 69, 118-119**
Miller, Scott,	**187**
money	
not a motivator,	**86, 89**
recognition,	**84**
shifts focus,	**85**
monitoring recognition process,	**169-171**
Morgan, Arthur E, quoted,	**163**
motivation,	**46**
movement and motivation,	**77-78**
Myths	
#1 Cash is the best recognition method,	**83-86**
#2 A salary is enough,	**87-90**
#3 Employee competition brings out the best in people,	**91-95**
#4 Only star performers deserve recognition,	**97-104**

N

Naisbitt, John, quoted,	**14**
negative reinforcement,	**12, 71-76**
Nelson, Bob, quoted,	**155**
network of workers,	**159-160**
Night on the Town,	**143**
Number Two,	**19**

O

O'Brien, Howard Vincent, quoted,	**173**
O'Dell, Carla, quoted,	**46, 60, 61**
opportunities for recognition,	**117-118**
organisations' needs,	**180**

P

Parker, Tom, quoted,	**15, 26, 27, 29, 30, 32, 44, 86, 92, 117**
parties,	**135, 141-143**

Index

Pavarotti, Luciano, quoted,	65
pay is never enough,	**83-84**
people	
as asset,	**30-31, 32**
as resource,	**20**
and see also employees	
personal contact,	**14**
personal contribution,	**28**
Peters, Tom, quoted,	**16, 102**
phone systems,	**17**
pilot process,	**156**
politics, internal,	**93-94**
Porras, Jerry I, quoted,	**25**
positive experiences,	**14**
positive interactions,	**14**
positive reinforcement,	**11, 19-20**
P/PC principle,	**15**
Prahalad, C K, quoted,	**87**
principles of reinforcers	
#1 positive reinforcer as a stimulus,	**65-66**
#2 quality varies,	**66**
#3 immediacy determines effectiveness,	**66-67**
#4 effectiveness varies by people,	**67**
#5 effectiveness varies with timing,	**67**
#6 intensity varies,	**67-68**
#7 recipients values differ,	**68**
#8 reinforcing progress rather than results,	**68-70**
#9 positive more effective than negative,	**70**
private acknowledgement,	**151**
procedure manual,	**158**
public acknowledgement,	**151**
publicity,	**135**
punishment,	**12, 71, 72, 73-74**
pursuit of needs,	**78**

Q

quality initiatives,	**160**

R

R & R system,	**59**
Raines, Claire, quoted,	**29, 33, 57, 90, 157**
Ralston, Dick,	**187**

Index

reading recommended,	**188-189**
receiving recognition,	**16, 153**
recipients valuation,	**128**
recognition	
definition,	**43**
emotional,	**16**
personal,	**16**
reward - not the same,	**59-63**
Recognition Survey form,	**36-40**
recognition systems	
abuse concerns,	**160, 170**
administrator,	**163-167**
appropriateness,	**55-56, 150**
automatic rewards,	**104**
behavior changes,	**75**
benefits package,	**103**
benefits, potential,	**173-174**
boring,	**102**
budget at high level,	**161-162**
candy system,	**136**
cash, impact of,	**84, 85-86**
celebrations,	**141-143**
change, driving,	**183**
characteristics of,	**132**
compensation substitute,	**102-103**
competition,	**63**
consistency,	**46-48, 149**
cost,	**33, 170-171**
developing a unique strategy,	**107**
documenting,	**152-153**
effective,	**12, 21, 35-40**
effectiveness criteria,	**104, 149-151**
employee benefit,	**11**
employee driven,	**128-129**
employee preferences,	**39**
employee satisfiers,	**89**
everyone has won,	**103**
evolutionary approach,	**155**
expert views and theories,	**77-79**
fairness,	**46-48, 149**
family inclusion,	**137**
flexibility,	**54-55, 129, 150**
formal,	**152**
frequency,	**51-53, 150**
funny money,	**133-134**
future rewards,	**79**

Index

gifts or gift certificates,	**134**
graduation ceremony,	**144**
I made a difference award,	**143-144**
immediacy,	**49-50, 85**
informal,	**152**
insincerity,	**104**
justice,	**48**
key questions,	**40**
lack of,	**29**
limousine service,	**144**
lottery,	**47, 63, 101**
management driven,	**46**
management requirements,	**169-171**
management training,	**28, 157-158**
meaning,	**43-58**
measuring results,	**156**
needs met by,	**30**
network,	**159-160**
newsletters,	**135**
Night on the Town,	**143**
non-cash long-lasting,	**84**
opportunities for recognition,	**117-118**
outside workplace examples,	**20-21**
parties,	**135, 141-143**
percentage recognised,	**60, 61, 91**
perception of insincerity,	**104**
performance requirements,	**39**
personal contribution,	**28**
pilot process,	**156**
practice valuation,	**39**
private acknowledgement,	**151**
procedure manual,	**158**
public acknowledgement,	**151**
publicity,	**135**
purpose,	**118**
quality initiatives,	**160**
receiver valuation,	**44**
recipients valuation of recognition,	**128**
relationships,	**39**
responsibility for,	**40, 119-120**
salary rises,	**103**
scientific evidence,	**65-70**
selecting awards,	**156-157**
sincerity,	**44-46, 102, 104, 149**
skeptics,	**162, 169**
special dress day,	**137**

specific,	**57, 151**
sponsorship at high level,	**158-159**
spontaneous,	**102**
sport cars,	**144**
stock options,	**103**
subjective judgement,	**63**
survey results,	**60-61**
team excellence awards,	**140-143**
thank you,	**16, 118, 120-121, 130-133, 150, 156**
thank you cards,	**130-133**
three A's,	**43-44**
tickets for special events,	**135**
time off,	**137**
timeliness,	**49-51, 150**
timely,	**102**
token	**133-134**
tools that are not recognition,	**101-104**
traveling trophy,	**136**
treasure chest,	**136**
types of acknowledgement,	**151-153**
types of recognitions,	**128-144**
universal use,	**129-131**
values list meaningless,	**25**
variety of recognitions,	**126**
verbal,	**152-153**
wall of fame,	**135**
what is being recognised,	**128**
written,	**152-153**
Reebok,	**136**
reinforcement methods research,	**11**
relationships	
building,	**15-20**
definition,	**17**
loyalty,	**15**
trust,	**15**
responsibility for recognition,	**119-120**
reward	
definition,	**59-61**
recognition - not the same,	**59-63**
Rice, Anne, quoted,	**149**
Ritz-Carlton Hotel,	**19**
Robert Half International, quoted,	**29**
Rosenthal, Robert, quoted,	**98**

Index

S

salary
dissatisfaction, 89
rises, 103
and see also cash
Scandinavian Airlines, 31
Schwab, Charles, quoted, 41
self-esteem, 61
Shafer, Leon and Helen, 186
sincerity, 44-46, 102, 104, 149
skeptics, 162, 169
Skinner, B F, 78-79
special dress day, 137
specificness, 57, 151
spirit, 86
sponsorship at high level, 158-159
spontaneity, 102
sport cars, 144
St Petersburg Times (Florida), quoted, 88
star performers, 97-104
Stefanski, Gene, 186
Stephens, Deborah C, quoted, 15, 26, 27, 29, 30, 32, 44, 86, 92, 117
stock options, 103
store exchanges, 18
strategy for development of unique recognition system
overview, 107
step 1 Determine what you want to achieve, 109-115
step 2 Identify what you will recognize, 117-126
step 3 Select your recognition tools, 127-144
step 4 Show you care, 149-153
Implementation, 155-162
Selecting the administrator, 163-1697
step 5 Measure, monitor and continuously improve your
recognition process, 169-171
subjective judgement, 63
success to be celebrated, 16
successful US companies, 25
Sunrise Consulting Group, quoted, 29, 31-32, 89

T

team excellence awards, 140-143
team working, 124

Index

teenagers,	17
Teresa, Mother, quoted,	51
Texas Restaurant Association,	30
thank you,	16, 118, 120-121, 130-133, 150, 156
3M,	94
tickets for special events,	135
time off,	137
timeliness,	49-51, 102, 150
tokens,	133-134
tokens of appreciation,	129
Townsend, Patrick, quoted,	49
traveling trophy,	136
Treacy, Michael, quoted,	127
treasure chest,	136
Twain, Mark, quoted,	59

U

United Airlines,	13-14
universal use of recognition,	129-130

V

values enthusiasm,	24
values loyalty,	24
Van Dyke, Henry, quoted,	91
verbal contracts,	115
verbal recognition,	152-153
Village Inn,	19

W

wall of fame,	135
Wall Street Journal, quoted,	29
Wall, Kathryn, quoted,	41
Watson, Thomas J Sr, quoted,	9, 101
Weight Watchers,	113
Western Electric,	88
Wiersema, Fred, quoted,	127
Wooden, John, quoted,	31
words, power of,	125
work load increases,	74
written recognition,	152-153

202